The Be Companion
Life and Rule of Saint Benedict

Prepared by Brother Hermenegild TOSF

Table of Contents

Introduction

The book, <u>The Benedict Option</u> by Rod Dreher calls on Christians to follow the spirit of Saint Benedict in living their lives. In fact, he calls for a new Saint Benedict to arise to bring about a reform of Christianity. He writes: "As we await a new Saint Benedict to appear in our quite different time and place and teach us how to reseave the tapestry of our Christian lives, ..." Let us pray that our wait will not be long. In fact these pages are dedicated to presenting Saint Benedict's life and rule to help all of live by Benedict's spirit.

He outlines the downward movement from sincere Christianity to the modern paganism, which reigns in the United States and in the world. He states: "We are living with the consequences of ideas accepted many generations ago, and as a result of those decisions, we are losing our religion..."

The truths of Christianity, which are found especially in the Sacred Scriptures, which inspired Saint Benedict are timeless. What was true two millenia ago is still true today. We should measure all modern teaching against the timeless truths of Christianity, rather than attempting to mold Christianity to the changing thinking of the world. As we read in Romans (12:1): "And be not conformed to this world; but be reformed in the newness of your mind, that you may prove what is the good, and the acceptable, and the perfect will of God."

Brother Hermenegild TOSF

Life of Saint Benedict

The Latin of this edition of the life of St. Benedict by St. Gregory the Great, is from that used by dom. Edmund Martàne, the English is almost exactly that of the quaint translation published in 1638. The test used for the Holy Rule is that of an ancient MS. existing at Monte Cassino, first published in 1659 by Dom. Paul de Ferrariis, a monk of that Abbey. The English is, as far as is consistent with the original, from the time honoured translation of 1638, as edited in 1875 by "one of the Benedictine Fathers of St. Michael's, near Hereford."

INTRODUCTION

There was a man of venerable life, Benedict by name and grace, who from the time of his very childhood carried the heart of an old man. His demeanour indeed surpassing his age, he gave himself no disport or pleasure, but living here upon earth he despised the world with all the glory thereof, at such time as he might have most freely enjoyed it. He was born in the province of Nursia of honourable parentage and sent to Rome to study the liberal sciences. But when he saw there many through the uneven paths of vice run headlong to their own ruin, he drew back his foot, lest, in the search of human knowledge, he might also fall into the same dangerous precipice. Contemning therefore learning and studies and abandoning his father's house and goods, he desired only to please God in a virtuous life. Therefore he departed skilfully ignorant and wisely unlearned. I have not attained unto all this man did, but the few things which I here set down, were related to me by four of his disciples; namely, Constantine, a very reverend man, who succeeded him in the government of the Monastery; Valentinian, who for many years bore rule in the Monastery of Lateran; Simplicius, who was the third superior of that congregation after him; and Honoratus who yet governeth the Monastery which he first inhabited.

CHAPTER I

Benedict having now left the schools resolved to betake himself to the desert, accompanied only by his nurse who most tenderly loved him. Coming therefore to a place called Affile, and remaining for some time in the Church of St. Peter by the charitable invitement of many virtuous people who lived there for devotion, so it chanced that his nurse borrowed of a neighbour a sieve to cleanse wheat, which being left carelessly upon the table was found broken in two pieces. Therefore on her return finding it broke, she began to weep bitterly because it was only lent her. But the religious and pious boy, Benedict, seeing his nurse lament was moved with compassion, and taking with him the two pieces of the broken sieve, with tears he gave himself to prayer, which no sooner ended, but he found the sieve whole, and found not any sign that it had been broken. Then presently he restored the sieve which had been broken, whole to his nurse, to her exceeding comfort. This matter was divulged unto all that lived thereabout, and so much admired by all, that the inhabitants of that place caused the sieve to be hanged up in the Church porch, that not only those present, but all posterity might know with how great gifts of grace Benedict had been endowed from the beginning of his conversion. The sieve remained to be seen for many years after, and hung over the Church door even until the times of the Longobards.

But Benedict more desirous to suffer afflictions than covetous of praise; and rather willing to undergo labours for the honour of God, than to be extolled with the favours of this world, fled secretly from his nurse to a remote place in the desert called Subiaco, distant about forty miles from Rome, in which a fountain springing with cool and crystal waters, extendeth itself at first into a broad lake, and running farther with increase of waters becometh at the last a river. As he was travelling to this place, a certain monk called Romanus met him and asked whither he was going. Having understood his intention, he both kept it secret and afforded him help, moreover he gave him a religious habit and assisted him in all things. The man of God being come to this place lived for the space of three years in an obscure cave, unknown to any man except Romanus the Monk, who lived not far off in a Monastery governed by Father Deodatus. But he would piously steal forth, and on certain days bring to Benedict a loaf of bread which he had spared from his own allowance. But there being no way to the cave from Romanus his cell by reason of a steep and high rock which hung over it, Romanus used to let down the loaf by a long cord to which also he fastened a little bell, that by the sound of it, the man of God might know when Romanus brought him the bread, and going out may receive it. But the old enemy, envying the charity of the one and the refection of the other, when on a certain day he beheld the bread let down in this manner, threw a stone and brake the bell. Notwithstanding, Romanus afterwards failed not to assist him in the best manner he was able. Now when it pleased Almighty God that Romanus should rest from his labours, and that the life of Benedict should be manifest to the world for an example to all men, that the candle set upon a candlestick might shine and give light to the whole Church of God, our Lord vouchsafed to appear to a certain Priest living far off, who had make ready his dinner for Easter Day, saying to him: "Thou hast prepared good cheer for thyself, and My servant in such a place is famished for hunger." Who presently rose up, and on the solemn day of Easter went towards the place with such meat as he had provided for himself, where seeking the man of God, amongst craggy rocks, winding valleys and hollow pits he found him hid in a cave. Then after prayers, and blessing the Almighty Lord, they sat down, and after some spiritual discourse the Priest said: "Rise, and let us take our refection, for this is Easter Day." To whom the man of God answered: "I know it is Easter, because I have found so much favour as to see thee." (For not having a long time conversed with men, he did not know it was Easter Day.) The good Priest did therefore again affirm it, saying: "Truly this is the day of our Lord's Resurrection, and therefore it is not fit that you should keep abstinence, and for this cause I am sent that we may eat together that which Almighty God hath bestowed on us." Whereupon blessing God, they fell to their meat. Their discourse and dinner ended, the Priest returned to his Church.

About the same time certain shepherds found him hid in a cave; who, at the first, spying him among the bushes, clothed in the skins of beasts, took him for some wild beast, but afterwards knowing him to be a servant of God, many of them were converted from their savage life to virtue. By this means his name began to be famous in the country, and many did resort unto him, bringing with them necessaries for his body, while they received from his lips the food of life.

How he overcame a temptation of the flesh

The holy man being on a certain day alone, the tempter was at hand; for a little black bird, commonly called an ousel, began to fly about his face, and that so near as the holy man, if he would, might have taken it with his hand; but no sooner had he made the sign of the cross than the bird vanished. When presently so great a carnal temptation assailed him, that before the holy man had never felt the like. For the remembrance of a woman which some time he had seen, was so lively represented to his fancy by the wicked spirit, and so vehemently did her image inflame his breast with lustful desires, that almost overcome by pleasure, he was determining to leave the wilderness. But suddenly assisted with divine grace he came to himself, and, seeing near him a thicket full of nettles and briars, he threw off his garments and cast himself naked into the midst of those sharp thorns and nettles, where he rolled himself so long, that, when he rose up, all his body was pitifully rent; thus by the wounds of his flesh he cured those of his soul, by turning pleasure into pain; and by the vehemence of outward torments he extinguished the unlawful flame which burnt within overcoming sin by changing the fire. After which time, as he himself related to his disciples, he was so free from the like temptation, that he never felt any such motion.

Many after this began to forsake the world and to hasten to put themselves under his government. Being now altogether free from vice, he worthily deserved to be made a master of virtue. As it is commanded by Moses that the Levites should serve from five and twenty years and upward, and after fifty years they should be appointed to keep the holy vessels.

PETER.

I have already understood something of this testimony alleged, yet I pray make it more plain unto me.

GREGORY.

It is manifest, Peter, that in youth the temptations of the flesh are great, but after fifty natural heat waxeth cold: now the souls of good men are the holy vessels. Therefore while the elect are in temptation, it is necessary that they live under obedience, and be wearied with labours, but when, by reason of their age, the fervour of temptations is assuaged, they are ordained keepers of holy vessels, that is become instructors of souls.

PETER.

I confess what you say has given me full satisfaction, and therefore this place of Scripture being clearly expounded, I pray you hasten on with the holy man's life which you have begun.

How St. Benedict broke a glass by the sign of the cross

Having thus vanquished this temptation, the man of God like a good soil well manured and weeded, brought forth abundant fruit of the seed of virtue, so that his fame began to spread itself more largely. Not far off was a Monastery, whose Abbot being dead, the whole Convent repaired to the venerable man Benedict, and with earnest persuasions requested him for their Abbot, which he refused for a long time, forewarning them that his manner of life and theirs were not agreeable; yet at length overcome with importunity he gave consent. But when in the same Monastery he began to observe regular discipline, so that none of the Monks (as in former time) were permitted by their disorder to swerve any way from the path of virtue, which receiving they fell into a great rage, and began accusing themselves of their choice in receiving him for a Superior, whose integrity of life was disproportionate to their perverseness.

And therefore, when they perceived themselves restrained from unlawful acts, it grieved them to leave their desires, and hard it was to relinquish old customs and begin a new life, besides the conversation of good men is always odious to the wicked, they began therefore to plot his death, and after consultation had together, they poisoned his wine. So when the glass which contained the empoisoned drink was, according to the custom of the Monastery, presented at table to be blessed by the Abbot, Benedict putting forth his hand and making the sign of the Cross, the glass which was held far off brake in pieces, as if instead of blessing the vase of death, he had thrown a stone against it. By this the man of God perceived that the glass had in it the drink of death which could not endure the sign of life. So presently rising up with a mild countenance and tranquil mind, having called the Brethren together, he thus spake unto them: "Almighty God of His mercy forgive you, Brethren, why have you dealt thus with me? Did not I foretell you that my manner of life and yours would not agree? Go, and seek a Superior to your liking; for you can have me no longer with you." This said, he forthwith returned to the solitude he loved so well, and lived there with himself, in the sight of Him who seeth all things.

PETER.

I do not well understand what you mean: "He lived with himself."

GREGORY.

If the holy man had been longer constrained to govern those who had unanimously conspired against him, and were so contrary to him in life and manners, it might, peradventure, have diminished his own vigour and fervour of devotion, withdrawing his mind from the light of contemplation. So that over much busied in correcting the faults of others, he might have neglected his own; and so perhaps lost himself, and yet not gained others. For as often as by contagious motions we are transported out of ourselves we remain the same, but not with ourselves, because not looking into our own actions, we are wandering about other things. For do we think that he was with himself who went into a far country, consumed the portion allotted to him, and, after he had put himself into the service of a citizen of that country, kept his hogs, and was glad to eat the husks which they are: notwithstanding, when he began to consider what he had lost, as the Scripture testifieth: "Being come to himself, he said: how many hirelings in my father's house have plenty of bread." If, therefore, he were before with himself, how was it true that he returned to himself?

I may well say, therefore, that his holy man lived with himself, because he never turned the eye of his soul from himself, but standing always on his guard with great circumspection, he kept himself continually in the all-seeing eye of his Creator.

PETER.

How is it then to be understood, which is written of the Apostle Peter, when he was led by the Angel out of the prison? Who returning to himself said: "Now I know assuredly that the Lord hath sent his

Angel, and hath delivered me out of the hands of Herod, and from all the expectation of the people of the Jews."

GREGORY.

Two ways, Peter, we are carried out of ourselves: for either by sinfulness of thought we fall beneath ourselves, or by the grace of contemplation we are raised above ourselves. He therefore, that kept the hogs, by his inconstancy of mind and uncleanness, fell beneath himself: but he, whom the Angel loosed and ravished into an ecstasy, was indeed out of himself, but yet above himself. But both of them returned to themselves, the one when, reclaiming his lewd life, he was converted at heart, the other when from the height of contemplation, he returned to his natural and ordinary understanding. Thus venerable Benedict in that solitude dwelt with himself, for as much as he kept himself within his thoughts: for as often as by the fervour of contemplation he was elevated, without doubt he left himself as it were beneath himself.

PETER.

I like well this you say but resolve me, I pray you, should he have left those Monks of whom he had once taken charge?

GREGORY.

In my opinion, Peter, a bad community may be tolerated where there are found at least some good which may be helped. But where there is no benefit to be expected of any good, labour is many times lost upon the bad. Especially if there be any present occasions wherein we may do God better service. Now whom was there whom the holy man should have stayed to govern, when they had all conspired against him? And many things are considered by the soul of the perfect which ought not to be passed in silence, for they, perceiving their endeavours to be without effect, depart to some other place, there to employ themselves more profitably. Wherefore that famous preacher who desired to be dissolved and to be with Christ, unto whom to live is Christ, and to die is gain, did not only desire himself to suffer, but did also animate others to do the like. He being persecuted at Damascus, caused himself to be let down from the wall by a cord and basket whereby he escaped privately. Shall we say then that Paul feared death which he earnestly desired for the love of Christ, as appeareth by his own testimony? But as he foresaw that his endeavours there would profit little, with much difficulty he reserved himself to labour in another place with better success. For this valiant champion of God would not be confined to so narrow limits, but sought battles in the open field. So you may observe that the venerable Benedict, left not so many incorrigible in that place as he converted to a spiritual life elsewhere.

PETER.

You say true, as both reason and the example alleged prove, but I pray return to prosecute the life of this holy Father.

GREGORY.

The holy man for many years in that desert increased wonderfully in virtues and miracles, whereby a great number in those parts were gathered together in the service of Almighty God: so that, by the assistance of our Lord Jesus Christ, he built there twelve monasteries, in each of which he put twelve Monks with their superiors, and retained a few with himself whom he thought to instruct further.

Now began divers noble and devout personages from Rome to resort to him, and commended their children to be brought up by him in the service of Almighty God. At the same time, Equitius brought unto him Maurus, and Tertullus a Senator his son Placidus, both very hopeful children, of which two, Maurus, although young, yet by reason of his forwardness in the school of virtue, began to assist his master, but Placidus was as yet a child of tender years.

How he reclaimed an indevout Monk

In one of those Monasteries which he had built thereabout, was a certain Monk that could not stay at his prayers, but, so soon as he saw his brethren kneel and dispose themselves for their mental prayer, he would go out, and there spend his wandering thoughts upon worldly and transitory things. For which, having been often admonished by his Abbot, he was brought before the man of God, who also sharply reprehended him for his folly; but, returning to his Monastery, he scarce remembered two days what the man of God had said to him, for the third day he fell to his old custom, and at the time of prayer went out again: whereof when the servant of God was informed by the Abbot the second time, he said: "I will come myself and reform him." And when he was come to the same Monastery, and the Brethren after the Psalms ended, at the accustomed time betook themselves to prayer, he perceived a little black boy, who pulled this Monk (who could not remain at his prayers) out by the hem of his garment. This he insinuated secretly to Pompeianus Abbot of the Monastery, and to Maurus: "See you not there who it is that draweth this Monk out?" Who answered, "No." "Let us pray", replied he, "that you may likewise see whom this Monk followeth." After prayer continued for two days, Maurus the monk saw, but Pompeianus the Abbot of the Monastery could not perceive anything. The next day when the man of God had finished his prayer he went out of the Oratory, and found the Monk standing without, whom he forthwith strake with a wand, and from that time ever after the Monk was free from the wicked suggestion of the black boy, and remained constant at his prayers. For the old enemy, as if himself had been beaten with the whip, dared no more to take command of his thoughts.

How by the prayer of the man of God a spring issued from the top of a mountain

Three of the Monasteries, which he founded in that place, were built upon the cliffs of a mountain, which was very troublesome to the Monks always to be forced to descend to the lake to fetch up their water, for, on account of the steepness of the mountain side, it was very difficult and dangerous to descend. Hereupon the Brethren of these three Monasteries came together to the servant of God Benedict saying: "It is very troublesome to us to have daily to go down for water as far as the lake, and therefore the Monasteries must of necessity be removed to some more commodious place." He dismissed them with comfortable words, and at night with little Placidus, whom we mentioned before, went up to the rock and there prayed a long time. Having ended his prayers, he put three stones for a mark in the same place, and so unknown to all he returned to his Monastery. Next day, when the Brethren came again to him for want of water he said: "Go, and on the rock where you shall find three stones one upon another, dig a little, for Almighty God is able to make water spring from the top of that mountain, that you may be eased of this labour."

When they had made a hollow in that place, it was immediately filled with water, which issueth forth so plentifully that to this day it continueth running down to the floor of the mountain.

How the iron head of a bill from the bottom of the water returned to the handle again

At another time, a certain Goth poor of spirit, desirous to lead a religious life, repaired to the man of God, Benedict, who most willingly received him. One day he ordered a bill to be given to him to cut up brambles in a place which he intended for a garden. This place, which the Goth had undertaken to accommodate, was over the lake's side. While the Goth labored in the cutting up the thick briars, the iron, slipping out of the handle, fell into the lake in a place so deep, that there was no hope to recover it. The Goth, having lost his bill, ran trembling to the Monk Maurus, and told him the mischance, confessing his fault penitently, who presently advised Benedict the servant of God thereof. Immediately the man of God came himself to the lake, took the haft out of the Goth's hand, and cast it into the lake, when, behold, the iron rose up from the bottom and entered into the haft as before. Which he there rendered to the Goth saying: "Behold! work on and be not discomforted."

How his disciple Maurus walked on the water

One day as venerable Benedict was in his cell, the aforesaid young Placidus, a Monk of the holy man, went out to the lake to fetch water, and letting down the bucket to take up water, by chance fell in himself after it, and was presently carried away by the stream, a bow's shoot from the side. This accident was at the same time revealed to the man of God in his cell, who quickly called Maurus, saying: "Run, brother Maurus, for the child who went to fetch water is fallen into the lake, and the stream hath carried him a great way." A wonderful thing and not heard of since the time of Peter the Apostle! Maurus having asked and received his benediction, upon the command of his Superior went forth in haste, and, being come to the place to which the child was driven by the stream, thinking still he went upon the dry land, he ran upon the water, took him by the hair of the head, and returned speedily back. No sooner had he set foot upon firm ground but he came to himself, and perceiving that he had gone upon the water, much astonished, he wondered how he had done that which wittingly he durst not adventure. So, returning to his Superior, he related what had happened, which the venerable man Benedict ascribed to Maurus his prompt obedience, and not to his own merits; but contrariwise Maurus attributed it wholly to his command, not imputing any virtue to himself in that which he had done unwittingly. This humble and charitable contention, the child who was saved, was to decide, for he said: "When I was drawn out of the water, methought I saw my Abbot's garments over my head and imagined that he had drawn me out."

PETER.

These are wonderful things you report, and may be to the edification of many: for my own part, the more I drink of this good man's miracles, the more I thirst.

Of the poisoned loaf which the crow carried away

When, as now, the places far and wide were very zealous in the love of our Lord God Jesus Christ, many abandoning the vanities of the world and putting themselves under the sweet yoke of our Redeemer; as it is the custom of the wicked to repine at the virtues of others, which themselves desire not to follow, one Florentius, the Priest of a Church hard by, and grandfather to Florentius our subdeacon, began by the instigation of the devil to be envious of the virtuous proceedings of the holy man, to derogate from his course of living hindering also as many as he could from resorting to him. But seeing that he could not stop his progress, the fame of his virtues still more increasing, and many upon the report of his sanctity reforming their lives daily, he became more and more envious, and constantly grew worse, for he desired himself the commendations of Benedict's life, but would not live commendably. Thus, blinded with envy, he sent to the servant of Almighty God a poisoned loaf for an offering, which the man of God received thankfully, although he was not ignorant of the poison in it. There used to come to him at the time of dinner a crow from the next forest, which took bread from his hand. Coming therefore, as she was wont, the man of God cast before her the bread that the Priest had sent him, saying: "In the name of the Lord Jesus Christ take this bread and cast it in some place where no man may find it." The crow, gaping and spreading her wings, run croaking about it, as though she would have said, I would willingly fulfil thy command, but I am not able. The man of God commanded again saying: "Take it up, take it up, and cast it where no man may find it." So at length the crow took it up in her beak and flew away with it and three hours after returned again to receive from his hand her ordinary allowance. But the venerable Father, seeing the Priest so perversely bent to seek his life, was more sorry for him than grieved for himself. When the aforesaid Florentius saw that he could not kill the body of his master, he attempted what he could against the souls of his disciples, in so much that he sent seven naked girls into the garden of the Cloister where Benedict lived, that so playing for a long time hand in hand, they might entice their souls to naughtiness, which when the holy man espied out of his cell, to prevent the fall of his younger disciples, and considering that all this was done only for the persecuting of himself, he gave place to envy, and after he had disposed of the Oratories and other buildings, leaving in them a competent number of Brethren with Superiors, he took with him a few monks and removed to another place. Thus the man of God with humility avoided his hatred, whom Almighty God struck with a terrible judgment: for when the aforesaid Priest, standing in his summer house, heard to his great joy, that Benedict was gone, the room wherein he was fell down and crushed and killed the enemy of Benedict, all the rest of the house remaining immovable. This Maurus, the disciple of the man of God, thought fit to signify forthwith to the venerable Father Benedict, who was yet scarce gone ten miles saying: "Return for the Priest that did persecute you is slain." Which the man of God hearing took very heavily, both because his enemy was dead and because his disciple rejoiced thereat. Whereupon he enjoined him a penance for presuming in a joyful manner to bring such news to him.

PETER.

These are wonderful strange things which thou sayest. For in the drawing water out of a rock methinks I behold in him Moses; in raising the iron from the bottom of the water he representeth Eliseus; in walking on the water Peter; in the obedience of the crow I conceive him another Elias; in bewailing his enemy's death I see David. In my opinion, this man was filled with the spirit of all the just.

GREGORY.

The man of God, Benedict, had in him, Peter, the spirit of God alone, which by the grace of free redemption replenished the hearts of all the elect, of which St. John saith: "There was true light which illuminateth every man that cometh into this world." Of which again it is written: "Of his plentitude and fulness we have all received." For the holy ones of God could indeed receive graces from God, but they could not impart them to others. He then gave signs of power to the lowly, who promised that He would shew the miracle of Jonas to His enemies, deigning in their sight to die, and in the sight of the humble to arise. So that the one should have what they would contemn, and the other what reverence and love. By which mystery it came to pass, that while the proud were spectators of His ignominious death, the humble contrariwise, against death, lay hold of the power of His glory.

PETER.

But declare, I pray, whither the holy man removed or if he wrought miracles in any other place?

GREGORY.

The holy man by removing changed his habitation, but not his adversary. For afterwards he endured so much the more grievous battles, by how much he had now the master of wickedness fighting openly against him. The castle called Cassino is situated upon the side of a high mountain, which containeth as it were, in the lap thereof, the same castle, and riseth into the air three miles high so that the top seemeth to touch the very heavens: on this stood an old temple where Apollo was worshipped by the foolish country people, according to the custom of the ancient heathens. Round about it, likewise, grew groves, in which even until that time, the mad multitude of infidels offered their idolatrous sacrifices. The man of God coming to that place brake down the idol, overthrew the altar, burnt the groves, and, of the temple of Apollo, made a chapel to St. Martin, and, where the profane altar had stood, he built a chapel of St. John; and, by continual preaching, converted many of the people thereabout. But the old enemy not bearing this silently, did present himself, not covertly or in a dream but openly and visibly in the sight of the Father, and with great cries complained of the violence he suffered, in so much that the brethren heard him though they could see nothing. For, as the venerable Father told his disciples, the wicked fiend represented himself to his sight all on fire, and, with flaming mouth and flashing eyes, seemed to rage against him. And, then, they all heard what he said, for, first, he called him by his name, and, when the man of God would make him no answer, he fell to reviling him. And whereas before he cried: "Benedict, Benedict," and saw he could get no answer, then he cried: "Maledict, not Benedict, what hast thou to do with me, and why dost thou persecute me?" But now we shall behold new assaults of the old enemy against the servant of God, against whom willingly did he make war, but against his will did he give him occasions of many victories.

How the man of God by his prayer, removed a huge stone

One day, as the brethren were building the cells of the Cloister, there lay a stone in the midst which they determined to lift up and put into the building. When two or three were not able to move it, they set more to it, but it remained as immoveable as if it had been held by roots to the ground, so that it was easy to conceive that the old enemy sat upon it, since that so many men were not able to lift it. After much labour in vain, they sent to the man of God to help them with his prayers to drive away the enemy, who presently came, and having first prayed, he gave his blessing, when behold the stone was as easily lifted as if it had not weight at all.

Of the fantastical fire which burned the kitchen

Then the man of God thought good that they should dig in that place. When they had entered a good deepness, the Brethren found a brazen idol, which happening for the present to be cast in the kitchen, suddenly there seemed a flame to rise out of it, and, to the sight of all the Monks it appeared that all the kitchen was on fire. As they were casting on water to quench this fire, the man of God, hearing the tumult, came, and perceiving that there appeared fire in the eyes of the Brethren and not in his, he forthwith bowed his head in prayer, and calling upon those whom he saw deluded with an imaginary fire, he bade them sign their eyes that they might behold the kitchen entire, and not those fantastical flames which the enemy had counterfeited.

How a boy crushed by the fall of a wall was healed by the servant of God

Again, when the Brethren were raising the wall a little higher for more convenience, the man of God was at his devotions in his cell, to whom the old enemy appeared in an insulting manner and told him he was going to his Brethren at work; the man of God straightway by a messenger advized the Brethren thereof saying: "Brethren, have a care of yourselves, for the wicked spirit at this hour is coming to molest you." Scarce had the messenger told his errand when the malignant spirit overthrew the wall that was abuilding, and with the fall thereof crushed a young monk, son to a certain Senator. Hereat all of them much grieved and discomforted, not for the loss of the wall but for the harm to their brother, brought the heavy tidings to their venerable Father Benedict, who bid them bring the boy to him, who could not be carried but in a sheet, by reason that not only his body was bruised but also his bones crushed with the fall. Then the man of God willed them to lay him in his cell upon his mat where he used to pray; so causing the Brethren to go out he shut the door, and with more than ordinary devotion fell to his prayers. A wonder to hear, the very same hour he sent him to his work again, whole and sound as ever he was before, to help his Brethren in making up the wall; whereas the old enemy hoped to have had occasion to insult Benedict for his death.

Of Monks who had eaten out of their monastery

Now began the man of God, by the spirit of prophecy, to foretell things to come, and to certify those that were present with him of things that passed far off. It was the custom of the Monastery that the Brethren, sent abroad about any business, should neither eat nor drink anything outside their Cloister. This in the practice of the Rule being carefully observed, one day some Brethren upon occasion went abroad, and were forced to stay later than usual, so they rested and refreshed themselves in the house of a certain devout woman of their acquaintance. Returning late to the Monastery, they asked, as was the custom, the Abbot's blessing, of whom he straightway demanded, saying: "Where dined you?" they answered: "Nowhere." To whom he said: "Why do you lie? Did you not go into such a woman's house? Eat you not there such and such meats? Drank you not so many cups?" When the venerable Father had told them both the woman's lodging, the several sorts of meats, with the number of their draughts, they, in great terror fell down at his feet, and with acknowledgment of all that they had done confessed their fault. But he straightway pardoned them, persuading himself they would never afterwards attempt the like in his absence knowing he was always present with them in spirit.

How he reproved the brother of Valentinian the Monk for eating by the way

Moreover, the brother of Valentinian, the Monk, whom we mentioned in the beginning, was very devout although but a secular; and he used to go to the Monastery from his dwelling once every year and that fasting, that he might partake of the prayers of the servant of God, and see his brother. As he was on his way to the Monastery, another traveller, who carried meat with him, put himself into his company After they had travelled a good while, he said to him: "Come, Brother, let us refresh ourselves, lest we faint by the way." "God forbid!" answered the other, "by no means, Brother, for my custom is always to go to the venerable Father Benedict fasting." At which answer, his fellow-traveller, for the present, said no more; but, when they had gone a little further, he moved him again to ear, but he would not consent because he resolved to keep his fast. So the other was awhile silent, and went forward with him without taking any thing himself. After they had gone a great way, wearied with long travel, in their way they came to a meadow and a spring, with what else might delight them, there to take their repast. Then said his fellow-traveller: "So! Here is water, here is a meadow, here is a pleasant place for us to refresh and rest us awhile, that we may safely make an end of our journey." So, at the third motion, these words pleasing his ear and the place his eye, he was overcome, consented and ate. In the evening he came to the Monastery, where, conducted to the venerable Father Benedict, he craved his prayers, but soon the holy man reproved him for what he had done in the way, saying: "What was it, Brother, the malignant enemy suggested to thee by they fellow traveller? The first time he could not persuade nor yet the second, but the third time he prevailed and obtained his desire." Then the man acknowledging his fault fell at his feet, and began all the more to weep and to be ashamed, by reason that he perceived he had offended, although absent, in the sight of Father Benedict.

PETER.

I discover in the breast of the holy man the spirit of Eliseus, who was present with his disciple though far from him.

How he discovered the dissimulation of King Totila

GREGORY.

You must, Peter, for a little while be silent, that you may know matters far more important. For, in the time of the Goths, their king, informed that the holy man had the gift of prophecy, went towards his Monastery and made some stay a little way off, and gave notice of his coming. To whom answer was made from the Monastery that he might come at his pleasure. The king, being of a treacherous nature, attempted to try whether the man of God had the spirit of prophecy. There was one of his guards called Riggo, upon whom he caused his own buskins to be put and so commanded him taking on him the king's person to go forward to the man of God, three of his chief pages attending upon him, to wit Vulderic, Ruderic and Blindin, to the end they should wait upon him in the presence of the servant of God, that so, by reason of his attendants and purple robes, he might be taken for the king. When the said Riggo, with his brave apparel and attendance, entered the cloister the man of God sat a little distance off, and seeing him come so nigh as he might hear him, he cried to him, saying: "Put off, son, put off that which thou carriest, for it is not thine." Riggo straightway fell to the ground and was much afraid, for having presumed to delude so holy a man; all his followers likewise fell down astonished, and rising, they durst not approach unto him, but returned to their king, and trembling related unto him how soon they were discovered.

How he prophesied to king Totila and to the Bishop of Canosa

Then Totila came himself to the man of God, whom as soon as he saw sitting afar off, he durst not come nigh, but fell prostrate to the ground. The holy man twice of three bade him rise, but he durst not get up, then Benedict, the servant of Jesus Christ our Lord, deigned himself to come to the prostrate king, whom, raising from the ground, he rebuked for his deeds, and foretold in a few words all that should befall him saying: "Much evil dost thou do, and much wickedness hast thou done, as least now give over thy iniquity. Into Rome shalt thou enter, thou wilt cross over the sea, nine years shalt thou reign, and die the tenth." At the hearing whereof, the king sore appalled, craved his prayers and departed, but from that time he was less cruel. Not long after he went to Rome, sailed thence to Sicily, and in the tenth year of his reign, by the judgment of Almighty God, lost both crown and life.

Moreover, the Bishop of the Church of Canosa used to come to the servant of God, who much loved him for his virtuous life. He, therefore, conferring with him concerning the coming of king Totila and the taking of the City of Rome, said: "The city doubtless will be destroyed by this king, so that it will never more be inhabited." To whom the man of God replied: "Rome shall never be destroyed by the Pagans, but shall be so shaken by tempests, lightnings and earthquakes that it will decay of itself." The mysteries of which prophecy we now behold as clear as day, for, in this city, we see the walls ruined, houses overturned, churches destroyed by tempestuous winds, and buildings rotten with old age, decay and falling into ruins. Although Honoratus, his disciple, from whose relation I had it, told me heard it not himself from his own mouth but was told it by the Brethren.

How venerable Benedict dispossessed a certain clerk from the Devil

At that time one of the clergy of the church of Aquin was molested with an evil spirit, whom the venerable man, Constantius, Bishop of that Diocese, had sent to divers martyrs' shrines to be cured; but the holy martyrs would not cure him, that the gifts of grace in Benedict might be made manifest. He was therefore brought to the servant of Almighty God, Benedict, who, by pouring forth prayers to our Lord Jesus Christ, presently drove out the enemy. Having cured him, he commanded him, saying: "Go! And hereafter never eat flesh, and presume not to take Holy Orders, for what time soever you shall presume to take Holy Orders, you shall again become a slave to the devil." The Clerk therefore went his way healed, and as present punishments make deep impressions, he carefully for a while observed the man of God's command. But when, after many years, all his seniors were dead and he saw his juniors preferred before him in Holy Orders, he neglected the words of the man of God, as though forgotten through length of time, and took upon him Holy Orders; whereupon, presently, the devil, who before had left him, took power of him, and never ceased to torment him till he severed his soul from his body.

PETER.

This holy man, I perceive, understood the secret decrees of God, in that he knew this Clerk to be delivered to the power of the devil, lest he should presume to receive Holy Orders.

GREGORY.

Why should not he know the secret decrees of Divine Providence, who kept the commandments of God, whence it is written that "he who adhereth to God is one spirit with Him."

PETER.

If he who adhereth to our Lord become one spirit with Him, how comes the same excellent Preacher to say: "Who hath known the mind of the Lord, or who has been His counsellor?" For it seems altogether unlikely that he, who is made one with another, should not know his mind.

GREGORY.

Holy men, so far as they are united with God, are not ignorant of His meaning, for the same Apostle saith; "For what man knoweth the things of a man, but the spirit of a man that is in him? So the things also, that are of God, no man knoweth but the spirit of God." And to shew that he knew things of God, he addeth: "But we have not received the spirit of this world, but the spirit which is of God." And again: "That eye hath not seen, nor ear heard, neither hath it ascended into the heart of man, what things God hath prepared for those that love Him, but to us God hath revealed by His spirit."

PETER.

If then those things which appertained to God were revealed to the said Apostle by the spirit of God, what meaneth he to make this preamble, saying: "O the depth of the riches of the wisdom and knowledge of God; how incomprehensible are His judgments and His ways unsearchable." But as I am saying this, another question arises: for the Prophet David says to our Lord: "With my lips I have uttered all the judgments of Thy mouth." And, whereas, it is less to comprehend or know than to pronounce, what is the reason that St. Paul should affirm the judgments of God to be incomprehensible, while David professeth not only to know them but also to pronounce them with his lips?

GREGORY.

To both these difficulties -- I briefly answered before, when I said: that holy men, as far as they are one with God, are not ignorant of the mind of our Lord, for all such as do devoutly follow the Lord are also by devotion one with God; and yet, in that they are laden with the burden of this corruptible flesh, they are not with God. Therefore, for as much as they are united with God they know His secret judgments, of which likewise they are ignorant for as much as in respect separated from Him: and so they pronounce His judgments incomprehensible which they cannot as yet thoroughly understand. But they who in spirit adhere to Him, in this adhesion know His judgments, either by the sacred words of Scripture, or by hidden revelations, as far as they are capable; these therefore they know and declare, but they are ignorant of those which God concealeth. Whereupon the prophet David when he had said: "In my lips I will pronounce all Thy judgments," as if he had said plainly: "Those judgments I could both know and pronounce which Thou didst tell me, for those which Thou speakest not, without doubt Thou concealest from our knowledge. Thus, the saying of the Prophet agreeth with that of the Apostle, for the judgments of God are both incomprehensible, and yet those which proceed from His mouth are uttered with the lips of men, for being so manifested by God they may be conceived by men, nor can they be concealed.

PETER.

By occasion of the difficulty I propounded, I have obtained a clear solution. But if there remain aught concerning the virtue of this man, I pray you declare it.

How he prophecied the destruction of his Monastery

A certain nobleman, named Theoprobus, was by the admonition of Father Benedict converted, and for the merit of his life was very familiar and intimate with him. He one day entered into the cell of the man of God, found him weeping bitterly; when he had waited a good while and saw he did not give over, (though it was his custom in prayer mildly to weep and not to use any doleful lamentations) he boldly demanded of him the cause of so great grief. To whom the man of God presently replied: "All this Monastery which I have built, with whatsoever I have prepared for my Brethren, are, by the judgment of Almighty God, delivered over to the heathen: and I could scarce obtain to save the lives of those in this place. His words Theoprobus heard, but we see them verified in the destruction of his Monastery by the Longobards. For of late these Lombards, by night, when the Brethren were at rest, entered the Monastery and ransacked all, yet had not the power to lay hand on any man. But Almighty God fulfilled what he had promised to His faithful servant, Benedict, that although he gave their goods into the hands of the Paynims, yet he preserved their lives. In this Benedict did most clearly resemble St. Paul, whose ship with all its goods being lost, yet, for his comfort, he had the lives of all that were in his company bestowed upon him.

How St. Benedict discovered the hiding of a flagon of wine

Our monk Exhilaratus, whom you know well, on a time was sent by his master with two wooden vessels (which we call flagons) full of wine, to the man of God in his Monastery. He brought one but hid the other in the way, notwithstanding, the man of God, although he was not ignorant of anything done in his absence, received it thankfully, and advised the boy as he was returning back, in this manner: "Take care, son, thou drink not of that flagon which thou hast hid, but turn the mouth of it downward and then thou wilt perceive what is in it." He departed from the holy man much ashamed, and desirous to make further trial of what he had heard, held the flagon downwards, and presently there came forth a snake, at which the boy was sore affrighted and terrified for the evil he had committed.

How the man of God reproved a Monk for receiving certain napkins

Not far distant from the monastery was a certain town in which no small number of people, by the exhortations of Benedict, were converted from the worship of idols to the faith of God. In that place were certain religious women, and the servant of God, Benedict, used to send often some of his Brethren thither to instruct and edify their souls. One day, as his custom was, he appointed one to go; but the Monk who was sent, after his exhortation, by the entreaty of the Nuns, took some small napkins and hid them in his bosom. As soon as he came back, the man of God began very sharply to rebuke him, saying: "How hath iniquity entered thy breast?" The Monk was amazed, and because he had forgotten what he had done, he wondered why he was so reprehended. To whom the holy Father said: "What! Was not I present when thou tookest the napkins of the handmaids of God and didst put them in thy bosom?" Whereupon he presently fell at his feet, and repenting of his folly threw away the napkins which he had hid in his bosom.

How the man of God understood the proud thought of one of his Monks

One day as the venerable Father late in the evening was at his repast, it happened that one of his Monks, the son of a lawyer, held the candle to him; and whilst the man of God was eating, he standing in that manner, began by the suggestion of pride to say within himself, "Who is he whom I should wait upon at table, or hold the candle unto with such attendance? Who am I who should serve him?" To whom the man of God presently turning, checked him sharply saying: "Sign thy breast, Brother, what is this you say? Sign thy breast." Then he forthwith called upon the Brethren and willed them to take the candle out of his hand, and bade him for that time to leave his attendance and sit down quietly by him. The Monk being asked afterward of the Brethren concerning his thoughts at that time, told them how he was puffed up with a spirit of pride, and what he spake against the man of God secretly in his own heart. By this it was easily to be perceived that nothing could be kept from the knowledge of venerable Benedict, in whose ears the words of unspoken thoughts resounded.

Of two hundred measures of meal found before the man of God's cell

At another time also in the country of Campania began a great famine, and all people suffered from great scarcity of food, so that all the wheat in Benedict's Monastery was spent, and likewise almost all the bread, so that but five loaves remained for the Brethren's refection.

When the venerable Father perceived them sad, he endeavoured by a mild and gentle reproach to reprehend their pusillanimity, and with fair promises to comfort them, saying: "Why is your soul sad for want of bread? To day you are in want but to-morrow you shall have plenty." The next day there were found two hundred sacks of meal before the Monastery gates, by whom God Almighty sent it as yet no man knoweth. Which when the Monks beheld, they gave thanks to God, and by this were taught in their greatest want to hope for plenty.

PETER.

Tell me, I pray you, is it to be thought that this servant of God had continually the spirit of prophecy, when himself pleased, or only at certain times with some discontinuance.

GREGORY.

The spirit of prophecy, Peter, doth not always cast his beams upon the understanding of the Prophets, for as it is written of the Holy Ghost: "He breatheth where He will." So likewise must we conceive, also, when He pleaseth. And, therefore, Nathan being asked by the king if he might build the Temple, first allowed him to do it, and afterwards forbade him. This was the reason that Eliseus knew not the cause why the woman wept but said to his servant who did oppose her: "Let her alone for her soul is in anguish, and the Lord hath concealed it from me and hath not made it known." Thus Almighty God of His great mercy so disposeth in His providence, for the end that by giving the spirit of prophecy sometimes, and at other times withdrawing it, the minds of the Prophets be both elevated above themselves, and also be kept in humility, for by receiving the spirit they may know they are inspired by God, and again they receive it not, they may consider what they are of themselves.

PETER.

It standeth with good reason what you have said. But, I beseech you, prosecute what else you remember of the venerable Father Benedict.

How by a vision, he gave order to construct The Monastery of Terracina

At another time, he was requested by a certain devout man to send some of his disciples to build a Monastery on his estate near the city of Terracina. To which request he consented, and sent some Monks, appointing an Abbot and Prior over them. As they were setting forward, he promised, saying: "Go, and upon such a day I will come and shew you where to build the Oratory, where the Refectory and lodging for the guests, or what else shall be necessary." So they received his blessing and departed, in hope to see him at the appointed day, for which they prepared all things they thought fit and necessary for their Father and his company. The night before the appointed day the man of God appeared in sleep to him whom he had constituted Abbot and to his Prior, and described to them most exactly how he would have the building ordered. When they awaked, they related to each other what they had seen, yet not altogether relying upon that vision, they expected the man of God according to his promise, but seeing he came not at his appointed time, they returned to him very pensive, saying: "We have expected, Father, your coming, as you promised, but you came not to shew us where and what we should build." To whom he said: "Why, Brethren, why do you say so? Did not I come according to my promise?" And when they said: "When came you?" he replied: "Did I not appear to each of you in your sleep and describe every place? Go, and according to the direction given you in that vision construct the Monastery." Hearing this they were much astonished, and so, returning to the manor, they erected the whole building according to the revelation.

PETER.

I would gladly be informed how and in what manner he could express his mind to them so far off, so they should both hear and understand by an apparition.

GREGORY.

What is the reason, Peter, thou dost so curiously search out the manner how it was done? It is evident that the spirit is of more mobile nature than the body. And we are taught by Scripture how the Prophet was taken up in Judea and set down, with the dinner he carried, in Chaldea, and, after he had refreshed another Prophet with his dinner, found himself again in Judea. If then Habacuc in a moment could corporally go so far and carry his dinner, what wonder if Father Benedict obtained to go in spirit and intimate to the spirits of his Brethren what was necessary; that as the other went corporally to convey corporal food, so he might go in spirit to inform them of things concerning a spiritual life?

PETER.

I confess that by this your discourse you have given full satisfaction to my doubtful mind; but I would gladly know what kind of man he was in his common conversation.

How certain Religious women were absolved After their death

GREGORY.

Even his ordinary discourse, Peter, had a certain efficacious virtue, for his heart being elevated in contemplation, he would not allow a word to pass from his mouth in vain. If at any time he spake aught, yet not as one that determined what was best to be done, but by way of threatening, his words had the same force as if he had absolutely decreed it. For, not far from his Monastery, two Nuns of noble race and parentage lived in a place of their own: and a certain Religious man provided them with all things for their exterior. But as in some, nobility of birth causeth baseness in mind, so those, who bear in mind their own greatness do less humble themselves in this world. There aforesaid Nuns had not, as yet, refrained their tongues by a Religious habit, but, by their unadvised speeches, oftentimes provoked to anger the Religious man who had care over them. Wherefore, after he had for a long time endured their contumelious language, he complained to the man of God of the injuries he suffered. Which as soon as he heard he commanded them forthwith, saying: "Have a care of your tongues, for if you do not amend I excommunicate you." Which sentence of excommunication notwithstanding, he did not pronounce but threaten. Yet for all this, they nothing changed in their former conditions. Within a few days after they departed this life, and were buried in the Church. At such time as a Solemn Mass was sung, and the Deacon, as the custom is, cried aloud: "If there be any that communicateth not, let him go forth," then their nurse, who used to make offerings to our Lord for them, saw them rise out of their graves and go forth. This she often observed, that, when the Deacon cried in that manner, they went out, not able to remain in the Church, and, calling to mind what the man of God had said to them whilst they were living, (for he excluded them from communion unless they amended their language and manners) she, with great sorrow, informed the servant of God what she had seen. He presently with his own hands gave the offering saying: "Go and cause this oblation to be offered to our Lord, and they shall be no longer excommunicated." When therefore, this offering was made, and the Deacon, according to custom, cried out that such as did not communicate should go out of the Church, they were not seen to go forth any more. Whereby it was apparent that, whereas they went not forth with the excommunicated, they were admitted by our Lord to communion.

PETER.

It is marvellous strange that this man, although venerable and most holy, as yet living in the mortal body, should be able to release those who were standing at the invisible tribunal.

GREGORY.

And was not he, Peter, yet in this flesh who heard; "Whatsoever thou shalt bind upon earth shall be bound also in Heaven, and whatsoever thou shalt loose on earth shall be loosed also in Heaven." Whose place and authority in binding and loosing they possess, who, by faith and virtuous life, obtain the dignity of holy government. And that man, an earthly creature, might receive this power, the Creator of Heaven and earth came down from Heaven to earth and that flesh might judge of spiritual things He became man for the redemption of mankind. For God thus condescending beneath Himself raised our weakness above itself.

PETER.

For the virtue of his miracles your words do yield a very good reason.

Of a boy who was cast out of his grave

GREGORY.

Upon a certain day, a young Monk of his, who was over-much affected towards his parents, went from the Monastery to their abode without his benediction, and the very same day, as soon as he was come to them he died. The day following his burial they found his body cast up, which they interred the second time, and the next day after it was found in like manner lying above ground as before. Hereupon they ran straight way and fell at the feet of the most mild Father Benedict imploring his aid, to whom the man of God with his own hand gave the communion of the Lord's Body saying: "Go, and lay the Body of the Lord upon his breast and so bury him." This done, the earth kept his body, and never after cast it up. You perceive, Peter, of what merit this man was with our Lord Jesus Christ, seeing that the very earth cast forth the body of him who had not received the blessing of Benedict.

PETER.

I do plainly perceive it, and am much astonished thereat.

Of the Monk, who leaving his Monastery met a dragon in the way

One of his Monks of a wandering and inconstant disposition, would by no means abide in the Monastery. Although the man of God had often reproved and admonished him of it, he would in no wise consent to remain in the congregation, and often entreated earnestly to be released. So the venerable Father, overcome with his importunity in anger bade him begone. Scarce was he got out of the Monastery, when he met in the way a dragon who, with open mouth made towards him. Seeing it ready to devour him, he began to quake and tremble, crying out aloud: "Help, help, for this dragon will devour me." The Brethren upon this ran out, yet saw no dragon, but took the panting and afrighted Monk back again to the Monastery, who forthwith promised never to depart and from that time he remained always constant in his promise. He, by the prayers of the holy man, was made to see the dragon ready to devour him, which before he had followed unperceived.

Of the boy cured of the Leprosy

But I must not pass over in silence what I heard of a very honourable man named Anthony, who affirmed that a servant of his father fell into a leprosy, insomuch that his hair fell off, and his skin was swollen so that he could no longer hide the increase of his disease. Who being sent by the gentleman's father to the man of God, he was by him quickly restored to his former health.

How St. Benedict miraculously procured money for a poor man to discharge his debt

Nor will I conceal that which his disciple Peregrine was wont to relate: how, on a certain day, an honest man, constrained by the necessity of a debt, thought his only remedy was to have recourse to the man of God, and acquaint him with his necessity. So he came to the Monastery, where finding the servant of Almighty God, told him how he was extremely urged by his creditor for the payment of twelve shillings. The venerable father answered him that, in very deed, he had not twelve shillings, but yet he comforted his want with good words, saying: "Go, and after two days return hither again for today I have it not to give thee." These two days, as his custom was, he spent in prayer, and, on the third day, when the poor debtor came again, thirteen shillings were found upon a chest of the Monastery that was full of corn. These the man of God caused to be brought to him, and gave them to the distressed man, saying that he might pay twelve, and have one to defray his charges.

But to return to those things which I learned of his disciples of whom I spoke in the beginning of this book, there was a certain man had an adversary who bore him deadly hatred, and so great was his malice that he gave him poison in his drink; which potion, although it procured not his death, yet so altered his colour that his body became all speckled like a leper. This man was brought to the man of God and was quickly restored to his former health; for as soon as he touched him, the diversity of colours vanished from his skin.

How a bottle was cast down upon the Stones and not broken

At such time as the great famine was in Campania, the man of God gave all he had in his Monastery to those in want, insomuch as there was almost nothing left in the cellar save only a little oil in a glass vessel. When one Agapitus, a Subdeacon, came earnestly entreating to have a little oil given him, the man of God (who had resolved to give all upon earth that he might have all in Heaven) commanded this little oil that was left to be given him. The Monk, who was Cellarer, heard his command but was loath to fulfill it. And the holy man a little while after demanded whether he had done what he willed him, and the Monk answered that he had not given it, because if he had given it, there would be nothing left for the Brothers. Hereat, much displeased, the good father bade some other take the glass bottle in which there remained a little oil, and cast it out of the window, to the end that nothing of the fruits of disobedience might remain in the Monastery. This was accordingly done; under the window was a steep fall, full of huge rough stones, upon which the glass fell, yet it remained as whole and entire as if it had not been thrown down, so that neither was the glass broke nor the oil spilt. Then the man of God commanded it to be taken up and given to him that asked it. Then calling the Brothers together, he rebuked the disobedient Monk before them all for his pride and unfaithfulness.

How an empty barrel was filled with oil

Having ended the Chapter, he and all the Brethren fell to their prayers. In the place where they prayed was an empty oil-barrel close covered. As the holy man continued his prayer, the cover of the said barrel began to be heaved up by the oil increasing under it, which ran over the brim of the vessel upon the floor in great abundance. Which so soon as the servant of God, Benedict, beheld, he forthwith ended his prayer, and the oil ceased to run over. Then he admonished the distrustful and disobedient brother to have confidence and learn humility. So the brother thus reprehended was much ashamed, because the venerable Father had by his admonition and by his miracle shewn the power of Almighty God, nor could anyone afterwards doubt of what he promised, since, as it were in a moment, for a glass bottle almost empty, he had restored a barrel full of oil.

How he delivered a Monk from the devil

One day as he was going to St. John's Oratory, which stands upon the very top of the mountain, he met the old enemy upon a mule, in the habit and comportment of a physician, carrying a horn and a mortar; who, being demanded whither he went, answered he was going to the monks to minister a potion. So the venerable Father Benedict went forward to the chapel to pray, and, having finished, returned back in great haste, for the wicked spirit found one of the ancient Monks drawing water, and presently he entered into him, threw him on to the ground and tortured him pitifully. As soon as the man of God, returning from prayer, found him thus cruelly tormented, he only gave him a blow on the cheek with his hand, and immediately drave the wicked spirit out of him, so that he durst never after return.

PETER.

I would know whether he obtained these great miracles always by prayer, or did them some times only by the intimation of his will?

GREGORY.

They who are perfectly united with God, when necessity requireth, work miracles both ways, sometimes they do wonders by prayer, sometimes by power. For since St. John saith: "As many as received Him, to them He gave power to become sons of God." What wonder is it if they have the privilege and power to work miracles who are exalted to the dignity of children of God. And that they work miracles in both ways is manifest in St. Peter, who by prayer, raised Tabitha from death, and punished with death Ananias and Sapphira for their falsehood. For we do not read that he prayed when they fell down dead, but only that he rebuked them for their fault committed. It is evident therefore that these things are done sometimes by power, sometimes by petition: since that by reproof he deprived these of their life, and by prayer revived the other. But now I will produce two other acts of the faithful servant of God, Benedict, in which it shall clearly appear that some things he could do by power received from Heaven, and others by prayer.

How a country man was loosed by only the sight of the man of God

A certain Goth named Galla was of the impious sect of the Arians, and he, in the time of their king Totila did, with such monstrous cruelty, persecute religious men of the Catholic Church, insomuch that if any cleric or monk came in his sight, he was sure not to escape from his hands alive. This man enraged with an insatiable covetousness of spoil and pillage, lighted one day upon a husbandman whom he tortured with cruel torments. The rustic, overcome with pain, professed that he had committed his goods to the custody of the servant of God, Benedict. This he feigned that he might free himself from torments and prolong his life for some time. Then this Galla gave over tormenting him, and tying his arms together with a strong cord, made him run before his horse to shew him who this Benedict was, that had received his goods. Thus the man went in front, having his arms bound, and brought him to the holy man's Monastery, whom he found sitting alone at the Monastery gate reading. Then the countryman said to Galla, who followed furiously after him: "See! This is Father Benedict whom I told you of." The barbarous ruffian, looking upon him with enraged fury, thought to affright him with his usual threats, and began to cry out with a loud voice, saying: "Rise, rise and deliver up this rustic's goods which thou hast received." At whose voice the man of God suddenly lifted up his eyes from reading, and saw him and also the countryman whom he kept bound: thus, as he cast his eyes upon his arms, in a wonderful manner the cords began to fall off so quickly, that no man could possibly have so soon untied them.

When Galla perceived the man whom he brought bound, so suddenly loosened and at liberty, struck into fear at the sight of so great power, he fell prostrate, and bowing his stiff and cruel neck at the holy man's feet, begged his prayers. But the holy man rose not from his reading but called upon the Brethren to bring him to receive his benediction. When he was brought to him, he exhorted him to leave his barbarous and inhuman cruelty. So, vanquished, he departed, never after presuming to ask anything of the countryman, whom the man of God unloosed not by touching but by casting his eye upon. Thus you see, Peter, as I said, that those who are the true servants of Almighty God, sometimes do work miracles by a commanding power, for he who sitting still abated the fury of that terrible Goth and with his only look unloosed the cords wherewith the innocent man's arms were fast pinioned, sheweth, evidently, by the swiftness of the miracle, that he wrought it by a power received. Now I will also shew you how great and strange a miracle he obtained by prayer.

How he raised a child from the dead

As he was one day in the field labouring with his Brethren, a certain peasant came to the Monastery, carrying in his arms the dead body of his son, and pitifully lamenting his loss, asked for the holy Father Benedict. When they said that he was in the field, he presently laid down the dead body of his son at the Monastery gate, and, as one distracted with grief, began running to find out the venerable father. At the same time the man of God was coming home with his Brethren from labouring in the field, whom, when the distressed countryman espied, he began to cry out: "Restore me my son, restore me my son." But the man of God amazed at this voice said: "What! have I taken your son from you?" To whom the man replied: "He is dead, come and raise him." When the servant of God heard this he was much grieved, and said: "Go, Brethren, go! This is not a work for us, but such as were the holy Apostles. Why will you impose burdens upon us which we cannot bear?" Notwithstanding, the man enforced with excessive grief, persisted in his petition, swearing that he would not depart unless he raised his son to life. Then the servant of God enquired, saying: "Where is he?" He answered: "Lo! his body lieth at the Monastery Gate." Whither, when the man of God with his Brethren was come, he knelt down and laid himself on the body of the child; then, raising himself and with his hands held up towards Heaven, he prayed: "O Lord, regard not my sins, but the faith of this man who craveth to have his son restored to life, and restore again to this body the soul which thou hast taken from it." Scarce had he finished these words, but all the body of the boy began to tremble at the re-entry of the soul, so that in the sight of all who were present he was seen with wonderful quaking to pant and breathe. Whom he presently took by the hand and delivered alive and sound to his father.

It seemeth to me, Peter, he had not this miracle actually in his power, which he prostrated himself to obtain by prayer.

PETER.

What you have said is undoubtedly true, because you prove by deeds what was said in words. But I pray, certify me, whether holy men can effect and obtain whatsoever they will or desire?

Of the miracle wrought by his sister Scholastica

GREGORY.

Who was ever, Peter, in this life more sublime than St. Paul, who, notwithstanding, three times craved of our Lord to be free from the pricks of the flesh, yet could not obtain it? To this purpose, I must tell you a passage concerning the venerable Father Benedict, that there was something he desired and was not able to accomplish.

His sister Scholastica, who was consecrated to God from her very childhood, used to come once a year to see him; unto whom the man of God was wont to go to a house not far from the gate, within the possession of the Monastery. Thither she came one day according to her custom, and her venerable brother likewise with his disciples: where, after they had spent the whole day in the praise of God and pious discourses, the night drawing on, they took their refection together. As they were yet sitting at table, and protracting the time with holy conference, the religious woman, his sister, entreated him saying: "I beseech you, leave me not this night, that we may talk until morning of the joys of the heavenly life." To whom he answered: "What is this you say, sister? By no means can I stay out of my Monastery." At this time the sky was serene, and not a cloud was to be seen in the air. The holy woman, therefore, hearing her brother's refusal, clasped her hands together upon the table, and bowing her head upon them she prayed to Almighty God. As she raised up her head from the table, there began such vehement lightning and thunder, with such abundance of rain, that neither venerable Benedict nor his Brethren were able to put foot out of doors. For the holy woman when she leaned her head upon her hands, poured forth a flood of tears upon the table by which she changed the fair weather into foul and rainy. For, immediately after her prayers, followed the inundation, and the two did so concur that, as she lifted up her head, the crack of thunder was heard, so that in one and the same instant she lifted up her head and brought down the rain. Then the man of God perceiving that, by reason of thunder and lightening with continual showers of rain, he could not possibly return to his monastery, was sad and began to complain, saying: "God Almighty forgive you, sister, what is this you have done?" To whom she made answer: "I prayed you to stay and you would not hear me; I prayed to Almighty God and He heard me! Now, therefore, if you can, go forth to the Monastery and leave me." But he not able to go forth, was forced to stay against his will.

Thus it fell out that they spent the night in watching, and received full content in spiritual discourse of heavenly matters. By this it appears, as I said before, that he desired something which he could not obtain; for if we consider the mind of the venerable man, he would, without doubt, have had the fair weather to continue in which he set out. But, contrary to what he willed, he found a miracle worked by the courage of a woman in the strength of Almighty God. And no wonder if at that time a woman were more powerful than he, considering she had long desired to see her brother. For according to the saying of St. John: "God is charity," and with good reason she was more powerful who loved more.

PETER.

I confess that I am wonderfully pleased with that which you tell me.

In what manner St. Benedict saw the soul Of his sister go forth from her body

GREGORY.

The next day, the venerable woman returned to her Cloister and the man of God to his Monastery. When, behold, three days after, while standing in his cell, he saw the soul of his sister depart out of her body, and, in the form of a dove, ascend and enter into the celestial mansions. Who rejoicing much to see her great glory, gave thanks to God Almighty in hymns and praises, and announced her death to the Brethren. Whom he forthwith sent to bring her body to the Monastery, and caused it to be buried in the same tomb that he had prepared for himself. By means of which it fell out, that as their minds were always one in God, so also their bodies were not separated in their burial.

How the whole world was represented before his Eyes: and the soul of Germanus, Bishop of Capua.

Another time, Servandus, Deacon and Abbot of that Monastery which was built by Liberius, sometime a senator, in the Campania, used often to visit him, for being also illuminated with grace and heavenly doctrine, he repaired divers times to the Monastery that they might mutually communicate one to another, and, at least with sighs and longing desires, taste of that sweet food of the celestial country whose perfect fruition they were not as yet permitted to enjoy. When it was time to go to rest, venerable Benedict went up to the top of the tower in the lower part of which Servandus the Deacon had his lodging, and from which there was an open passage to ascend to the higher. Over against the said tower was a large building in which the disciples of both reposed. While as yet the Monks were at rest, the man of God, Benedict, being diligent in watching, rose up before the night office and stood at the window making his prayer to Almighty God about midnight, when suddenly, looking forth, he saw a light glancing from above, so bright and resplendent that it not only dispersed the darkness of the night, but shined more clear than the day itself. Upon this sight a marvellous strange thing followed, for, as he afterwards related, the whole world, compacted as it were together, was represented to his eyes in one ray of light. As the venerable Father had his eyes fixed upon this glorious lustre, he beheld the soul of Germanus, Bishop of Capua, carried by angels to Heaven in a fiery globe. Then, for the testimony of so great a miracle, with a loud voice he called upon Servandus the Deacon, twice or thrice by his name, who, troubled at such an unusual crying out of the man of God, came up, looked forth, and saw a little stream of light then disappearing, and wondered greatly at this miracle. Whereupon the man of God told him in order all that he had seen, and sent presently to Theoprobus, a Religious man in the town of Cassino, ordering him to go the same night to Capua, and learn what had happened to Germanus the Bishop. It fell out so, that he who was sent found the most reverend Bishop Germanus dead, and on enquiring more exactly, he learned that his departure was the very same moment in which the man of God had seen him ascend.

PETER.

A wonderful thing and much to be admired, but, whereas you said that the whole world, as it were, under one sunbeam, was represented to his sight, as I never experienced the like, so I cannot imagine how or in what manner this was possible that the whole world should be seen of any one man.

GREGORY.

Assure yourself, Peter, of that which I speak: that in a soul that beholdeth the Creator, all creatures appear but narrow; for, should we partake never so little of the light of the Creator, whatsoever is created would seem very little; because the soul is enlarged by this Beatific vision, and so dilated in the Divine perfections, that it far transcends the world and itself also. The soul thus rapt in the light of God is in her interior lifted up, and enabled above itself, and while thus elevated it contemplates itself, and it easily comprehendeth how little that is which before it was not able to conceive. So the blessed man who saw the globe of fire with the Angels returning to Heaven could not possibly have beheld those things but only in the light of God. What wonder then if he saw the world at one view who was in mind exalted above the world? But whereas I said that the whole world compacted as it were together was represented before his eyes, it is not meant that heaven and earth were straitened by contraction, but that the mind of the beholder was dilated, which, rapt in the sight of God might, without difficulty, see all that is under God. Therefore, in that light which appeared to his outward eyes, the inward light which was in his soul ravished the mind of the beholder with higher things, and shewed how mean are all inferior things.

PETER.

I perceive that it was to my profit that I understood you not before, for my slowness has been the occasion of so long and profitable a discourse. But, since you have clearly explained these things to me, I beseech you continue your former narration.

How he wrote a Rule for Monks

I would willingly, Peter, relate many things concerning this venerable Father, but some of purpose I omit, because I hasten to speak of the acts of others. Only this I would not have you to be ignorant of, that the man of God, among so many miracles wherewith he shined to the world, was also eminent for his doctrine, for he wrote a Rule for Monks both excellent for discretion and eloquent in style. Of whose life and conversation if any wish to know further, he may in the institution of that Rule understand all his manner of life and discipline, for the holy man could not possibly teach otherwise than he lived.

How he prophetically foretold his death

To his Brethren.

The same year in which he departed out of this life, he foretold the day of his most holy death to some of his disciples who conversed with him, and to others who were far off; giving strict charge to those who were present to keep in silence what they had heard, and declaring to the absent by what sign they should know when his soul departed out of his body. Six days before his departure he caused his grave to be opened, and immediately after he fell into a fever, by the violence whereof his strength began to wax faint, and the infirmity daily increasing, the sixth day he caused his disciples to carry him into the Oratory, where he did arm himself for his going forth by receiving the Body and Blood of the Lord; then, supporting his weak limbs by the hands of his disciples, he stood up, his hands lifted towards Heaven, and with words of prayer at last breathed forth his soul. The same day two of his Brethren, the one living in the Monastery and the other in a place far remote, had a revelation in one and the self-same manner. For they beheld a way, spread with garments and shining with innumerable lamps, stretching directly eastwards from his cell up to Heaven; a man of venerable aspect stood above and asked them whose way that was. But they professing they knew not, he said to them: "This is the way by which the beloved of the Lord, Benedict, ascended." Thus the disciples who were present knew of the death of the holy man, and so also those who were absent understood it by the sign foretold them. He was buried in the Oratory of St. John the Baptist which he himself had built upon the ruins of Apollo's altar.

How a mad woman was cured in his cave

In the cave also in which he formerly lived in Subiaco, even to this day, miracles are wrought upon such as repair thither with true faith. For very lately happened that which I now relate. A certain woman bereft of reason, and altogether distracted in her senses, roamed over mountains and valleys, through woods and fields by day and night, never resting, except when forced from weariness to lie down. One day, as she raged thus madly up and down, she lighted upon the cave of blessed Benedict, and by chance entered and remained there. The next morning she came out as sound and perfect in her senses as if she had never been out of them, and from that time remained all her life in the health which she had there recovered.

PETER.

What should be the reason that we experience, even in the patronage of martyrs, that they do not bestow so great favours by their bodies as by their relics: yea, and do greater miracles where themselves be not?

GREGORY.

Where the bodies of holy martyrs lie, no doubt, Peter, but there they are able to shew many miracles, as they do; for to such as have recourse unto them, with pure mind, they shew many marvellous favours. But forasmuch as weak souls might doubt whether they be present to hear them or no in those places where their bodies be not, it is necessary to shew more miracles where weak souls may doubt of their presence. For they whose minds are fixed in God have so much the greater merit of faith, that though their bodies lie not there, yet they be there present to hear our prayers. Wherefore Truth Itself to increase the faith of His disciples said: "If I go not away the Paraclete will not come unto you." For whereas it is certain, that the Holy Ghost, the Comforter, always proceedeth from the Father and the Son: why doth the Son say that He will go from them that the Paraclete may come, who never departeth from the Son? But because the Disciples beholding our Lord in the flesh, did desire always to behold Him with their corporeal eyes, it was rightly said unto them: "Unless I go away the Paraclete will not come." As if He had said plainly: If I withdraw not My bodily presence, I do not shew you the love of the Spirit: and, unless you cease to see Me carnally, you will never learn to love spiritually.

PETER.

What you say pleaseth me.

GREGORY.

Let us now for a while cease our discourse, that by silence we may be the better enabled to prosecute the miracles of other saints.

THE END.

48

Rule of Saint Benedict

Saint Benedict, Abbot of Monte Cassino
Translated by Verheyen, Rev. Boniface (1844-1923)

Table of Contents

PROLOGUE

Listen, O my son, to the precepts of thy master, and incline the ear of thy heart, and cheerfully receive and faithfully execute the admonitions of thy loving Father, that by the toil of obedience thou mayest return to Him from whom by the sloth of disobedience thou hast gone away.

To thee, therefore, my speech is now directed, who, giving up thine own will, takest up the strong and most excellent arms of obedience, to do battle for Christ the Lord, the true King.

In the first place, beg of Him by most earnest prayer, that He perfect whatever good thou dost begin, in order that He who hath been pleased to count us in the number of His children, need never be grieved at our evil deeds. For we ought at all times so to serve Him with the good things which He hath given us, that He may not, like an angry father, disinherit his children, nor, like a dread lord, enraged at our evil deeds, hand us over to everlasting punishment as most wicked servants, who would not follow Him to glory.

Let us then rise at length, since the Scripture arouseth us, saying: "It is now the hour for us to rise from sleep" (Rom 13:11); and having opened our eyes to the deifying light, let us hear with awestruck ears what the divine voice, crying out daily, doth admonish us, saying: "Today, if you shall hear his voice, harden not your hearts" (Ps 94[95]:8). And again: "He that hath ears to hear let him hear what the Spirit saith to the churches" (Rev 2:7). And what doth He say? —"Come, children, hearken unto me, I will teach you the fear of the Lord" (Ps 33[34]:12). "Run whilst you have the light of life, that the darkness of death overtake you not" (Jn 12:35). And the Lord seeking His workman in the multitude of the people, to whom He proclaimeth these words, saith again: "Who is the man that desireth life and loveth to see good days" (Ps 33[34]:13)? If hearing this thou answerest, "I am he," God saith to thee: "If thou wilt have true and everlasting life, keep thy tongue from evil, and thy lips from speaking guile; turn away from evil and do good; seek after peace and pursue it" (Ps 33[34]:14-15). And when you shall have done these things, my eyes shall be upon you, and my ears unto your prayers. And before you shall call upon me I will say: "Behold, I am here" (Is 58:9).

What, dearest brethren, can be sweeter to us than this voice of the Lord inviting us? See, in His loving kindness, the Lord showeth us the way of life. Therefore, having our loins girt with faith and the performance of good works, let us walk His ways under the guidance of the Gospel, that we may be found worthy of seeing Him who hath called us to His kingdom (cf 1 Thes 2:12).

If we desire to dwell in the tabernacle of His kingdom, we cannot reach it in any way, unless we run thither by good works. But let us ask the Lord with the Prophet, saying to Him: "Lord, who shall dwell in Thy tabernacle, or who shall rest in Thy holy hill" (Ps 14[15]:1)?

After this question, brethren, let us listen to the Lord answering and showing us the way to this tabernacle, saying: "He that walketh without blemish and worketh justice; he that speaketh truth in his heart; who hath not used deceit in his tongue, nor hath done evil to his neighbor, nor hath taken up a reproach against his neighbor" (Ps 14[15]:2-3), who hath brought to naught the foul demon tempting him, casting him out of his heart with his temptation, and hath taken his evil thoughts whilst they were yet weak and hath dashed them against Christ (cf Ps 14[15]:4; Ps 136[137]:9); who fearing the Lord are not puffed up by their goodness of life, but holding that the actual good which is in them cannot be done by themselves, but by the Lord, they praise the Lord working in them (cf Ps 14[15]:4), saying with the Prophet: "Not to us, O Lord, not to us; by to Thy name give glory" (Ps 113[115:1]:9). Thus also the Apostle Paul hath not taken to himself any credit for his preaching, saying: "By the grace of God, I am what I am" (1 Cor 15:10). And again he saith: "He that glorieth, let him glory in the Lord" (2 Cor 10:17).

Hence, the Lord also saith in the Gospel: "He that heareth these my words and doeth them, shall be likened to a wise man who built his house upon a rock; the floods came, the winds blew, and they beat upon that house, and it fell not, for it was founded on a rock" (Mt 7:24-25).

The Lord fulfilling these words waiteth for us from day to day, that we respond to His holy admonitions by our works. Therefore, our days are lengthened to a truce for the amendment of the misdeeds of our present life; as the Apostle saith: "Knowest thou not that the patience of God leadeth thee to penance" (Rom 2:4)? For the good Lord saith: "I will not the death of the sinner, but that he be converted and live" (Ezek 33:11).

Now, brethren, that we have asked the Lord who it is that shall dwell in His tabernacle, we have heard the conditions for dwelling there; and if we fulfil the duties of tenants, we shall be heirs of the kingdom of heaven. Our hearts and our bodies must, therefore, be ready to do battle under the biddings of holy obedience; and let us ask the Lord that He supply by the help of His grace what is impossible to us by nature. And if, flying from the pains of hell, we desire to reach life everlasting, then, while there is yet time, and we are still in the flesh, and are able during the present life to fulfil all these things, we must make haste to do now what will profit us forever.

We are, therefore, about to found a school of the Lord's service, in which we hope to introduce nothing harsh or burdensome. But even if, to correct vices or to preserve charity, sound reason dictateth anything that turneth out somewhat stringent, do not at once fly in dismay from the way of salvation, the beginning of which cannot but be narrow. But as we advance in the religious life and faith, we shall run the way of God's commandments with expanded hearts and unspeakable sweetness of love; so that never departing from His guidance and persevering in the monastery in His doctrine till death, we may by patience share in the sufferings of Christ, and be found worthy to be coheirs with Him of His kingdom.

CHAPTER I
Of the Kinds or the Life of Monks

It is well known that there are four kinds of monks. The first kind is that of Cenobites, that is, the monastic, who live under a rule and an Abbot.

The second kind is that of Anchorites, or Hermits, that is, of those who, no longer in the first fervor of their conversion, but taught by long monastic practice and the help of many brethren, have already learned to fight against the devil; and going forth from the rank of their brethren well trained for single combat in the desert, they are able, with the help of God, to cope single-handed without the help of others, against the vices of the flesh and evil thoughts.

But a third and most vile class of monks is that of Sarabaites, who have been tried by no rule under the hand of a master, as gold is tried in the fire (cf Prov 27:21); but, soft as lead, and still keeping faith with the world by their works, they are known to belie God by their tonsure. Living in two's and three's, or even singly, without a shepherd, enclosed, not in the Lord's sheepfold, but in their own, the gratification of their desires is law unto them; because what they choose to do they call holy, but what they dislike they hold to be unlawful.

But the fourth class of monks is that called Landlopers, who keep going their whole life long from one province to another, staying three or four days at a time in different cells as guests. Always roving and never settled, they indulge their passions and the cravings of their appetite, and are in every way worse than the Sarabaites. It is better to pass all these over in silence than to speak of their most wretched life.

Therefore, passing these over, let us go on with the help of God to lay down a rule for that most valiant kind of monks, the Cenobites.

CHAPTER II
What Kind of Man the Abbot Ought to Be

The Abbot who is worthy to be over a monastery, ought always to be mindful of what he is called, and make his works square with his name of Superior. For he is believed to hold the place of Christ in the monastery, when he is called by his name, according to the saying of the Apostle: "You have received the spirit of adoption of sons, whereby we cry Abba (Father)" (Rom 8:15).

Therefore, the Abbot should never teach, prescribe, or command (which God forbid) anything contrary to the laws of the Lord; but his commands and teaching should be instilled like a leaven of divine justice into the minds of his disciples.

Let the Abbot always bear in mind that he must give an account in the dread judgment of God of both his own teaching and of the obedience of his disciples. And let the Abbot know that whatever lack of profit the master of the house shall find in the sheep, will be laid to the blame of the shepherd. On the other hand he will be blameless, if he gave all a shepherd's care to his restless and unruly flock, and took all pains to correct their corrupt manners; so that their shepherd, acquitted at the Lord's judgment seat, may say to the Lord with the Prophet: "I have not hid Thy justice within my heart. I have declared Thy truth and Thy salvation" (Ps 39[40]:11). "But they contemning have despised me" (Is 1:2; Ezek 20:27). Then at length eternal death will be the crushing doom of the rebellious sheep under his charge.

When, therefore, anyone taketh the name of Abbot he should govern his disciples by a twofold teaching; namely, he should show them all that is good and holy by his deeds more than by his words; explain the commandments of God to intelligent disciples by words, but show the divine precepts to the dull and simple by his works. And let him show by his actions, that whatever he teacheth his disciples as being contrary to the law of God must not be done, "lest perhaps when he hath preached to others, he himself should become a castaway" (1 Cor 9:27), and he himself committing sin, God one day say to him: "Why dost thou declare My justices, and take My covenant in thy mouth? But thou hast hated discipline, and hast cast My words behind thee" (Ps 49[50]:16-17). And: "Thou who sawest the mote in thy brother's eye, hast not seen the beam in thine own" (Mt 7:3).

Let him make no distinction of persons in the monastery. Let him not love one more than another, unless it be one whom he findeth more exemplary in good works and obedience. Let not a free-born be preferred to a freedman, unless there be some other reasonable cause. But if from a just reason the Abbot deemeth it proper to make such a distinction, he may do so in regard to the rank of anyone whomsoever; otherwise let everyone keep his own place; for whether bond or free, we are all one in Christ (cf Gal 3:28; Eph 6:8), and we all bear an equal burden of servitude under one Lord, "for there is no respect of persons with God" (Rom 2:11). We are distinguished with Him in this respect alone, if we are found to excel others in good works and in humility. Therefore, let him have equal charity for all, and impose a uniform discipline for all according to merit.

For in his teaching the Abbot should always observe that principle of the Apostle in which he saith: "Reprove, entreat, rebuke" (2 Tm 4:2), that is, mingling gentleness with severity, as the occasion may call for, let him show the severity of the master and the loving affection of a father. He must sternly rebuke the undisciplined and restless; but he must exhort the obedient, meek, and patient to advance in virtue.

But we charge him to rebuke and punish the negligent and haughty. Let him not shut his eyes to the sins of evil-doers; but on their first appearance let him do his utmost to cut them out from the root at once, mindful of the fate of Heli, the priest of Silo (cf I Kings 2:11-4:18). The well-disposed and those of good understanding, let him correct at the first and second admonition only with words; but let him chastise the wicked and the hard of heart, and the proud and disobedient at the very first offense with stripes and other bodily punishments, knowing that it is written: "The fool is not corrected with words" (Prov 29:19).

And again: "Strike thy son with the rod, and thou shalt deliver his soul from death" (Prov 23:14).

The Abbot ought always to remember what he is and what he is called, and to know that to whom much hath been entrusted, from him much will be required; and let him understand what a difficult and arduous task he assumeth in governing souls and accommodating himself to a variety of characters. Let him so adjust and adapt himself to everyone—to one gentleness of speech, to another by reproofs, and to still another by entreaties, to each one according to his bent and understanding—that he not only suffer no loss in his flock, but may rejoice in the increase of a worthy fold. Above all things, that the Abbot may not neglect or undervalue the welfare of the souls entrusted to him, let him not have too great a concern about fleeting, earthly, perishable things; but let him always consider that he hath undertaken the government of souls, of which he must give an account.

And that he may not perhaps complain of the want of earthly means, let him remember what is written: "Seek ye first the kingdom of God and His justice, and all these things shall be added unto you" (Mt 6:33). And again: "There is no want to them that fear Him" (Ps 33[34]:10). And let him know that he who undertaketh the government of souls must prepare himself to give an account for them; and whatever the number of brethren he hath under his charge, let him be sure that on judgment day he will, without doubt, have to give an account to the Lord for all these souls, in addition to that of his own. And thus, whilst he is in constant fear of the Shepherd's future examination about the sheep entrusted to him, and is watchful of his account for others, he is made solicitous also on his own account; and whilst by his admonitions he had administered correction to others, he is freed from his own failings.

CHAPTER III
Of Calling the Brethren for Counsel

Whenever weighty matters are to be transacted in the monastery, let the Abbot call together the whole community, and make known the matter which is to be considered. Having heard the brethren's views, let him weigh the matter with himself and do what he thinketh best. It is for this reason, however, we said that all should be called for counsel, because the Lord often revealeth to the younger what is best. Let the brethren, however, give their advice with humble submission, and let them not presume stubbornly to defend what seemeth right to them, for it must depend rather on the Abbot's will, so that all obey him in what he considereth best. But as it becometh disciples to obey their master, so also it becometh the master to dispose all things with prudence and justice. Therefore, let all follow the Rule as their guide in everything, and let no one rashly depart from it.

Let no one in the monastery follow the bent of his own heart, and let no one dare to dispute insolently with his Abbot, either inside or outside the monastery. If any one dare to do so, let him be placed under the correction of the Rule.

Let the Abbot himself, however, do everything in the fear of the Lord and out of reverence for the Rule, knowing that, beyond a doubt, he will have to give an account to God, the most just Judge, for all his rulings. If, however, matters of less importance, having to do with the welfare of the monastery, are to be treated of, let him use the counsel of the Seniors only, as it is written: "Do all things with counsel, and thou shalt not repent when thou hast done" (Sir 32:24).

CHAPTER IV
The Instruments of Good Works

(1) In the first place to love the Lord God with the whole heart, the whole soul, the whole strength...(2) Then, one's neighbor as one's self (cf Mt 22:37-39; Mk 12:30-31; Lk 10:27).(3) Then, not to kill...(4) Not to commit adultery...(5) Not to steal...(6) Not to covet (cf Rom 13:9).(7) Not to bear false witness (cf Mt 19:18; Mk 10:19; Lk 18:20). (8) To honor all men (cf 1 Pt 2:17).(9) And what one would not have done to himself, not to do to another (cf Tob 4:16; Mt 7:12; Lk 6:31). (10) To deny one's self in order to follow Christ (cf Mt 16:24; Lk 9:23).(11) To chastise the body (cf 1 Cor 9:27).(12) Not to seek after pleasures.(13) To love fasting.(14) To relieve the poor.(15) To clothe the naked... (16) To visit the sick (cf Mt 25:36).(17) To bury the dead. (18) To help in trouble.(19) To console the sorrowing.(20) To hold one's self aloof from worldly ways.(21) To prefer nothing to the love of Christ.(22) Not to give way to anger.(23) Not to foster a desire for revenge.(24) Not to entertain deceit in the heart.(25) Not to make a false peace.(26) Not to forsake charity.(27) Not to swear, lest perchance one swear falsely.(28) To speak the truth with heart and tongue. (29) Not to return evil for evil (cf 1 Thes 5:15; 1 Pt 3:9).(30) To do no injury, yea, even patiently to bear the injury done us.(31) To love one's enemies (cf Mt 5:44; Lk 6:27). (32) Not to curse them that curse us, but rather to bless them.(33) To bear persecution for justice sake (cf Mt 5:10).(34) Not to be proud...(35) Not to be given to wine (cf Ti 1:7; 1 Tm 3:3).(36) Not to be a great eater. (37) Not to be drowsy.(38) Not to be slothful (cf Rom 12:11).(39) Not to be a murmurer. (40) Not to be a detractor.(41) To put one's trust in God. (42) To refer what good one sees in himself, not to self, but to God. (43) But as to any evil in himself, let him be convinced that it is his own and charge it to himself.(44) To fear the day of judgment.(45) To be in dread of hell.(46) To desire eternal life with all spiritual longing. (47) To keep death before one's eyes daily.(48) To keep a constant watch over the actions of our life.(49) To hold as certain that God sees us everywhere.(50) To dash at once against Christ the evil thoughts which rise in one's heart.(51) And to disclose them to our spiritual father.(52) To guard one's tongue against bad and wicked speech.(53) Not to love much speaking.(54) Not to speak useless words and such as provoke laughter.(55) Not to love much or boisterous laughter.(56) To listen willingly to holy reading.(57) To apply one's self often to prayer.(58) To confess one's past sins to God daily in prayer with sighs

and tears, and to amend them for the future.(59) Not to fulfil the desires of the flesh (cf Gal 5:16).(60) To hate one's own will. (61) To obey the commands of the Abbot in all things, even though he himself (which Heaven forbid) act otherwise, mindful of that precept of the Lord: "What they say, do ye; what they do, do ye not" (Mt 23:3).(62) Not to desire to be called holy before one is; but to be holy first, that one may be truly so called.(63) To fulfil daily the commandments of God by works.(64) To love chastity.(65) To hate no one.(66) Not to be jealous; not to entertain envy.(67) Not to love strife.(68) Not to love pride.(69) To honor the aged.(70) To love the younger.(71) To pray for one's enemies in the love of Christ.(72) To make peace with an adversary before the setting of the sun.(73) And never to despair of God's mercy.

Behold, these are the instruments of the spiritual art, which, if they have been applied without ceasing day and night and approved on judgment day, will merit for us from the Lord that reward which He hath promised: "The eye hath not seen, nor the ear heard, neither hath it entered into the heart of man, what things God hath prepared for them that love Him" (1 Cor 2:9). But the workshop in which we perform all these works with diligence is the enclosure of the monastery, and stability in the community.

CHAPTER V
Of Obedience

The first degree of humility is obedience without delay. This becometh those who, on account of the holy subjection which they have promised, or of the fear of hell, or the glory of life everlasting, hold nothing dearer than Christ. As soon as anything hath been commanded by the Superior they permit no delay in the execution, as if the matter had been commanded by God Himself. Of these the Lord saith: "At the hearing of the ear he hath obeyed Me" (Ps 17[18]:45). And again He saith to the teachers: "He that heareth you heareth Me" (Lk 10:16).

Such as these, therefore, instantly quitting their own work and giving up their own will, with hands disengaged, and leaving unfinished what they were doing, follow up, with the ready step of obedience, the work of command with deeds; and thus, as if in the same moment, both matters—the master's command and the disciple's finished work—are, in the swiftness of the fear of God, speedily finished together, whereunto the desire of advancing to eternal life urgeth them. They, therefore, seize upon the narrow way whereof the Lord saith: "Narrow is the way which leadeth to life" (Mt 7:14), so that, not living according to their own desires and pleasures but walking according to the judgment and will of another, they live in monasteries, and desire an Abbot to be over them. Such as these truly live up to the maxim of the Lord in which He saith: "I came not to do My own will, but the will of Him that sent Me" (Jn 6:38).

This obedience, however, will be acceptable to God and agreeable to men then only, if what is commanded is done without hesitation, delay, lukewarmness, grumbling or complaint, because the obedience which is rendered to Superiors is rendered to God. For He Himself hath said: "He that heareth you heareth Me" (Lk 10:16). And it must be rendered by the disciples with a good will, "for the Lord loveth a cheerful giver (2 Cor 9:7). " For if the disciple obeyeth with an ill will, and murmureth, not only with lips but also in his heart, even though he fulfil the command, yet it will not be acceptable to God, who regardeth the heart of the murmurer. And for such an action he acquireth no reward; rather he incurreth the penalty of murmurers, unless he maketh satisfactory amendment.

CHAPTER VI
Of Silence

Let us do what the Prophet saith: "I said, I will take heed of my ways, that I sin not with my tongue: I have set a guard to my mouth, I was dumb, and was humbled, and kept silence even from good things" (Ps 38[39]:2-3). Here the prophet showeth that, if at times we ought to refrain from useful speech for the sake of silence, how much more ought we to abstain from evil words on account of the punishment due to sin.

Therefore, because of the importance of silence, let permission to speak be seldom given to perfect disciples even for good and holy and edifying discourse, for it is written: "In much talk thou shalt not escape sin" (Prov 10:19). And elsewhere: "Death and life are in the power of the tongue" (Prov 18:21). For it belongeth to the master to speak and to teach; it becometh the disciple to be silent and to listen. If, therefore, anything must be asked of the Superior, let it be asked with all humility and respectful submission. But coarse jests, and idle words or speech provoking laughter, we condemn everywhere to eternal exclusion; and for such speech we do not permit the disciple to open his lips.

CHAPTER VII
Of Humility

Brethren, the Holy Scripture crieth to us saying: "Every one that exalteth himself shall be humbled; and he that humbleth himself shall be exalted" (Lk 14:11; 18:14).

Since, therefore, it saith this, it showeth us that every exaltation is a kind of pride. The Prophet declareth that he guardeth himself against this, saying: "Lord, my heart is not puffed up; nor are my eyes haughty. Neither have I walked in great matters nor in wonderful things above me" (Ps 130[131]:1).

What then? "If I was not humbly minded, but exalted my soul; as a child that is weaned is towards his mother so shalt Thou reward my soul" (Ps 130[131]:2).

Hence, brethren, if we wish to reach the greatest height of humility, and speedily to arrive at that heavenly exaltation to which ascent is made in the present life by humility, then, mounting by our actions, we must erect the ladder which appeared to Jacob in his dream, by means of which angels were shown to him ascending and descending (cf Gen 28:12). Without a doubt, we understand this ascending and descending to be nothing else but that we descend by pride and ascend by humility. The erected ladder, however, is our life in the present world, which, if the heart is humble, is by the Lord lifted up to heaven. For we say that our body and our soul are the two sides of this ladder; and into these sides the divine calling hath inserted various degrees of humility or discipline which we must mount.

The first degree of humility, then, is that a man always have the fear of God before his eyes (cf Ps 35[36]:2), shunning all forgetfulness and that he be ever mindful of all that God hath commanded, that he always considereth in his mind how those who despise God will burn in hell for their sins, and that life everlasting is prepared for those who fear God. And whilst he guardeth himself evermore against sin and vices of thought, word, deed, and self-will, let him also hasten to cut off the desires of the flesh.

Let a man consider that God always seeth him from Heaven, that the eye of God beholdeth his works everywhere, and that the angels report them to Him every hour. The Prophet telleth us this when he showeth God thus ever present in our thoughts, saying: "The searcher of hearts and reins is God" (Ps 7:10). And again: "The Lord knoweth the thoughts of men" (Ps 93[94]:11) And he saith: "Thou hast understood my thoughts afar off" (Ps 138[139]:3). And: "The thoughts of man shall give praise to Thee" (Ps 75[76]:11).

Therefore, in order that he may always be on his guard against evil thoughts, let the humble brother always say in his heart: "Then I shall be spotless before Him, if I shall keep myself from iniquity" (Ps 17[18]:24). We are thus forbidden to do our own will, since the Scripture saith to us: "And turn away from thy evil will" (Sir 18:30). And thus, too, we ask God in prayer that His will may be done in us (cf Mt 6:10). We are, therefore, rightly taught not to do our own will, when we guard against what Scripture saith: "There are ways that to men seem right, the end whereof plungeth into the depths of hell" (Prov 16:25). And also when we are filled with dread at what is said of the negligent: "They are corrupted and become abominable in their pleasure" (Ps 13[14]:1). But as regards desires of the flesh, let us believe that God is thus ever present to us, since the Prophet saith to the Lord: "Before Thee is all my desire" (Ps 37[38]:10). We must, therefore, guard thus against evil desires, because death hath his station near the entrance of pleasure. Whence the Scripture commandeth, saying: "Go no after thy lusts" (Sir 18:30). If, therefore, the eyes of the Lord observe the good and the bad (cf Prov 15:3) and the Lord always looketh down from heaven on the children of men, to see whether there be anyone that understandeth or seeketh God (cf Ps 13[14]:2); and if our actions are reported to the Lord day and night by the angels who are appointed to watch over us daily, we must ever be on our guard, brethren, as the Prophet saith in the psalm, that God may at no time see us "gone aside to evil and become unprofitable" (Ps 13[14]:3), and having spared us in the present time, because He is kind and waiteth for us to be changed for the better, say to us in the future: "These things thou hast done and I was silent" (Ps 49[50]:21).

The second degree of humility is, when a man loveth not his own will, nor is pleased to fulfill his own desires but by his deeds carrieth our that word of the Lord which saith: "I came not to do My own will but the will of Him that sent Me" (Jn 6:38). It is likewise said: "Self-will hath its punishment, but necessity winneth the crown."

The third degree of humility is, that for the love of God a man subject himself to a Superior in all obedience, imitating the Lord, of whom the Apostle saith: "He became obedient unto death" (Phil 2:8).

The fourth degree of humility is, that, if hard and distasteful things are commanded, nay, even though injuries are inflicted, he accept them with patience and even temper, and not grow weary or give up, but hold out, as the Scripture saith: "He that shall persevere unto the end shall be saved" (Mt 10:22). And again: "Let thy heart take courage, and wait thou for the Lord" (Ps 26[27]:14). And showing that a faithful man ought even to bear every disagreeable thing for the Lord, it saith in the person of the suffering: "For Thy sake we suffer death all the day long; we are counted as sheep for the slaughter" (Rom 8:36; Ps 43[44]:22). And secure in the hope of the divine reward, they go on joyfully, saying: "But in all these things we overcome because of Him that hath loved us" (Rom 8:37). And likewise in another place the Scripture saith: "Thou, O God, hast proved us; Thou hast tried us by fire as silver is tried; Thou hast brought us into a net, Thou hast laid afflictions on our back" (Ps 65[66]:10-11). And to show us that we ought to be under a Superior, it continueth, saying: "Thou hast set men over our heads" (Ps 65[66]:12). And fulfilling the command of the Lord by patience also in adversities and injuries, when struck on the one cheek they turn also the other; the despoiler of their coat they give their cloak also; and when forced to go one mile they go two (cf Mt 5:39-41); with the Apostle Paul they bear with false brethren and "bless those who curse them" (2 Cor 11:26; 1 Cor 4:12).

The fifth degree of humility is, when one hideth from his Abbot none of the evil thoughts which rise in his heart or the evils committed by him in secret, but humbly confesseth them. Concerning this the Scripture exhorts us, saying: "Reveal thy way to the Lord and trust in Him" (Ps 36[37]:5). And it saith further: "Confess to the Lord, for He is good, for His mercy endureth forever" (Ps 105[106]:1; Ps 117[118]:1). And the Prophet likewise saith: "I have acknowledged my sin to Thee and my injustice I have not concealed. I said I will confess against myself my injustice to the Lord; and Thou hast forgiven the wickedness of my sins" (Ps 31[32]:5).

The sixth degree of humility is, when a monk is content with the meanest and worst of everything, and in all that is enjoined him holdeth himself as a bad and worthless workman, saying with the Prophet: "I am brought to nothing and I knew it not; I am become as a beast before Thee, and I am always with Thee" (Ps 72[73]:22-23).

The seventh degree of humility is, when, not only with his tongue he declareth, but also in his inmost soul believeth, that he is the lowest and vilest of men, humbling himself and saying with the Prophet: "But I am a worm and no man, the reproach of men and the outcast of the people" (Ps 21[22]:7). "I have been exalted and humbled and confounded" (Ps 87[88]:16). And also: "It is good for me that

Thou hast humbled me, that I may learn Thy commandments" (Ps 118[119]:71,73).

The eighth degree of humility is, when a monk doeth nothing but what is sanctioned by the common rule of the monastery and the example of his elders.

The ninth degree of humility is, when a monk withholdeth his tongue from speaking, and keeping silence doth not speak until he is asked; for the Scripture showeth that "in a multitude of words there shall not want sin" (Prov 10:19); and that "a man full of tongue is not established in the earth" (Ps 139[140]:12).

The tenth degree of humility is, when a monk is not easily moved and quick for laughter, for it is written: "The fool exalteth his voice in laughter" (Sir 21:23).

The eleventh degree of humility is, that, when a monk speaketh, he speak gently and without laughter, humbly and with gravity, with few and sensible words, and that he be not loud of voice, as it is written: "The wise man is known by the fewness of his words."

The twelfth degree of humility is, when a monk is not only humble of heart, but always letteth it appear also in his whole exterior to all that see him; namely, at the Work of God, in the garden, on a journey, in the field, or wherever he may be, sitting, walking, or standing, let him always have his head bowed down, his eyes fixed on the ground, ever holding himself guilty of his sins, thinking that he is already standing before the dread judgment seat of God, and always saying to himself in his heart what the publican in the Gospel said, with his eyes fixed on the ground: "Lord, I am a sinner and not worthy to lift up mine eyes to heaven" (Lk 18:13); and again with the Prophet: "I am bowed down and humbled exceedingly" (Ps 37[38]:7-9; Ps 118[119]:107).

Having, therefore, ascended all these degrees of humility, the monk will presently arrive at that love of God, which being perfect, casteth out fear (1 Jn 4:18). In virtue of this love all things which at first he observed not without fear, he will now begin to keep without any effort, and as it were, naturally by force of habit, no longer from the fear of hell, but from the love of Christ, from the very habit of good and the pleasure in virtue. May the Lord be pleased to manifest all this by His Holy Spirit in His laborer now cleansed from vice and sin.

CHAPTER VIII
Of the Divine Office during the Night

Making due allowance for circumstances, the brethren will rise during the winter season, that is, from the calends of November till Easter, at the eighth hour of the night; so that, having rested till a little after midnight, they may rise refreshed. The time, however, which remains over after the night office (Matins) will be employed in study by those of the brethren who still have some parts of the psalms and the lessons to learn.

But from Easter to the aforesaid calends, let the hour for celebrating the night office (Matins) be so arranged, that after a very short interval, during which the brethren may go out for the necessities of nature, the morning office (Lauds), which is to be said at the break of day, may follow presently.

CHAPTER IX
How Many Psalms Are to Be Said at the Night Office

During the winter season, having in the first place said the verse: Deus, in adjutorium meum intende; Domine, ad adjuvandum me festina, there is next to be said three times, Domine, labia mea aperies, et os meum annuntiabit laudem tuam (Ps 50[51]:17). To this the third psalm and the Gloria are to be added.

After this the 94th psalm with its antiphon is to be said or chanted.

Hereupon let a hymn follow, and after that six psalms with antiphons. When these and the verse have been said, let the Abbot give the blessing. All being seated on the benches, let three lessons be read alternately by the brethren from the book on the reading stand, between which let three responsories be said. Let two of the responsories be said without the Gloria, but after the third lesson, let him who is chanting say the Gloria. When the cantor beginneth to sing it, let all rise at once from their seats in honor and reverence of the Blessed Trinity.

Let the inspired books of both the Old and the New Testaments be read at the night offices, as also the expositions of them which have been made by the most eminent orthodox and Catholic Fathers.

After these three lessons with their responsories, let six other psalms follow, to be sung with Alleluia. After these let the lessons from the Apostle follow, to be said by heart, then the verse, the invocation of the litany, that is, Kyrie eleison.

And thus let the night office come to an end.

CHAPTER X
How the Office Is to Be Said during the Summer Season

From Easter till the calends of November let the whole psalmody, as explained above, be said, except that on account of the shortness of the nights, no lessons are read from the book; but instead of these three lessons, let one from the Old Testament be said from memory. Let a short responsory follow this, and let all the rest be performed as was said; namely, that never fewer than twelve psalms be said at the night office, exclusive of the third and the 94th psalm.

CHAPTER XI
How the Night Office Is to Be Said on Sundays

For the night office on Sunday the monks should rise earlier. At this office let the following regulations be observed, namely: after six psalms and the verse have been sung, as we arranged above, and all have been properly seated on the benches in their order, let four lessons with their responsories be read from the book, as we said above. In the fourth responsory only, let the Gloria be said by the chanter, and as soon as he beginneth it let all presently rise with reverence.

After these lessons let six other psalms with antiphons and the verse follow in order as before. After these let there be said three canticles from the Prophets, selected by the Abbot, and chanted with Alleluia. When the verse also hath been said and the Abbot hath given the blessing, let four other lessons from the New Testament be read in the order above mentioned.

But after the fourth responsory let the Abbot intone the hymn Te Deum laudamus. When this hath been said, let the Abbot read the lesson from the Gospel, all standing with reverence and awe. When the Gospel hath been read let all answer Amen, and immediately the Abbot will follow up with the hymn Te decet laus, and when he hath given the blessing Lauds will begin. Let this order of the night office be observed on Sunday the same way in all seasons, in summer as well as in winter, unless perchance (which God forbid) the brethren should rise too late and part of the lessons or the responsories would have to be shortened. Let every precaution be taken that this does not occur. If it should happen, let him through whose neglect it came about make due satisfaction for it to God in the oratory.

CHAPTER XII
How Lauds Are to Be Said

At Lauds on Sunday, let the 66th psalm be said first simply, without an antiphon. After that let the 50th psalm be said with Alleluia; after this let the 117th and the 62d be said; then the blessing and the praises, one lesson from the Apocalypse, said by heart, a responsory, the Ambrosian hymn, the verse and the canticle from the Gospel, the litany, and it is finished.

CHAPTER XIII
How Lauds Are to Be Said on Week Days

On week days let Lauds be celebrated in the following manner, to wit: Let the 66th psalm be said without an antiphon, drawing it out a little as on Sunday, that all may arriver for the 50th, which is to be said with an antiphon. After this let two other psalms be said according to custom; namely, the 5th and the 35th on the second day, the 42d and the 56th on the third day, the 63rd and the 64th on the fourth day, the 87th and the 89th on the fifth day, the 75th and the 91st on the sixth day, and on Saturday the 142d and the canticle of Deuteronomy, which should be divided into two Glorias. On the other days, however, let the canticle from the Prophets, each for its proper day, be said as the Roman Church singeth it. After these let the psalms of praise follow; then one lesson from the Apostle, to be said from memory, the responsory, the Ambrosian hymn, the verse, the canticle from the Gospel, the litany, and it is finished.

Owing to the sandals which are wont to spring up, the morning and the evening office should, plainly, never end unless the Lord's Prayer is said in the hearing of all by the Superior in its place at the end; so that in virtue of the promise which the brethren make when they say, "Forgive us as we forgive" (Mt 6:12), they may cleanse themselves of failings of this kind.

At the other hours which are to be said, however, let only the last part of this prayer be said aloud, so that all may answer, "But deliver us from evil" (Mt 6:13).

CHAPTER XIV
How the Night Office Is to Be Said on the Feasts of the Saints

On the feasts of the saints and on all solemn festivals let the night office be performed as we said it should be done on Sunday; except that the psalms, the antiphons, and the lessons proper for that day be said; but let the number above mentioned be maintained.

CHAPTER XV
At What Times the Alleluia Is to Be Said

From holy Easter until Pentecost let the Alleluia be said without intermission, both with the psalms and with the responsories; but from Pentecost until the beginning of Lent let it be said every night at the nocturns with the six latter psalms only. However, on all Sundays outside of Lent, let the canticles, Lauds, Prime, Tierce, Sext, and None be said with Alleluia. Let Vespers, however, be said with the antiphon; but let the responsories never be said with Alleluia, except from Easter to Pentecost.

CHAPTER XVI
How the Work of God Is to Be Performed during the Day

As the Prophet saith: "Seven times a day I have given praise to Thee" (Ps 118[119]:164), this sacred sevenfold number will be fulfilled by us in this wise if we perform the duties of our service at the time of Lauds, Prime, Tierce, Sext, None, Vespers, and Complin; because it was of these day hours that he hath said: "Seven times a day I have given praise to Thee" (Ps 118[119]:164). For the same Prophet saith of the night watches: "At midnight I arose to confess to Thee" (Ps 118[119]:62). At these times, therefore, let us offer praise to our Creator "for the judgments of His justice;" namely, at Lauds, Prime, Tierce, Sext, None, Vespers, and Complin; and let us rise at night to praise Him (cf Ps 118[119]:164, 62).

CHAPTER XVII
How Many Psalms Are to Be Sung at These Hours

We have now arranged the order of the psalmody for the night and the morning office; let us next arrange for the succeeding Hours. At the first Hour let three psalms be said separately, and not under one Gloria. Let the hymn for the same Hour be said after the verse Deus, in adjutorium (Ps 69[70]:2), before the psalms are begun. Then, after the completion of three psalms, let one lesson be said, a verse, the Kyrie eleison, and the collects.

At the third, the sixth, and the ninth Hours, the prayer will be said in the same order; namely, the verse, the hymn proper to each Hour, the three psalms, the lesson, the verse, the Kyrie eleison, and the collects. If the brotherhood is large, let these Hours be sung with antiphons; but if small, let them be said without a break.

Let the office of Vespers be ended with four psalms and antiphons; after these psalms a lesson is to be recited, next a responsory, the Ambrosian hymn, a verse, the canticle from the Gospel, the litany, the Lord's Prayer, and the collects.

Let Complin end with the saying of three psalms, which are to be said straight on without an antiphon, and after these the hymn for the same Hour, one lesson, the verse, Kyrie eleison, the blessing, and the collects.

CHAPTER XVIII
In What Order the Psalms Are to Be Said

In the beginning let there be said the verse, Deus, in adjutorium meum intende; Domine, ad adjuvandum me festina (Ps 69[70]:2), and the Gloria, followed by the hymn for each Hour. At Prime on Sunday, then, there are to be said four sections of the 118th psalm. At the other Hours, however, namely Tierce, Sext, and None, let three sections of the same psalm be said. But at Prime on Monday let three psalms be said, namely, the first, the second, and the sixth; and thus each day at Prime until Sunday, let three psalms be said each time in consecutive order up to the 19th psalm, yet so that the ninth psalm and the 17th be each divided into two Glorias; and thus it will come about that at the night office on Sundays we always begin with the 20th psalm.

At Tierce, Sext, and None, on Monday, however, let the nine sections which remain over the 118th psalm be said, three sections at each of these Hours. The 118th psalm having thus been parceled out for two days, namely, Sunday and Monday, let there be sung on Tuesday for Tierce, Sext, and None, three psalms each, from the 119th to the 127th, that is, nine psalms. These psalms will always be repeated at the same Hours in just the same way until Sunday, observing also for all these days a regular succession of the hymns, the lessons, and the verses, so, namely, that on Sunday the beginning is always made with the 118th psalm.

Let Vespers be sung daily with the singing of four psalms. Let these psalms begin with the 109th to the 147th, excepting those which are set aside for the other Hours; namely, from the 117th to the 127th, and the 133d, and the 142d. All the rest are to be said at Vespers; and as the psalms fall three short, those of the aforesaide psalms which are found to be longer, are to be divided; namely, the 138th, the 143d, and the 144th. But because the 116th is short, let it be joined to the 115th. The order of the psalms for Vespers having thus been arranged let the rest, namely, the lessons, the responsories, the hymns, the verses, and the canticles, be said as we have directed above.

At Complin, however, let the same psalms be repeated every day; namely, the 4th, the 90th, and the 133d.

Having arranged the order of the office, let all the rest of the psalms which remain over, be divided equally into seven night offices, by so dividing such of them as are of greater length that twelve fall to each night. We especially impress this, that, if this distribution of the psalms should perchance displease anyone, he arrange them if he thinketh another better, by all means seeing to it that the whole Psalter of one hundred and fifty psalms be said every week, and that it always start again from the beginning at Matins on Sunday; because those monks show too lax a service in their devotion who in the course of a week chant less than the whole Psalter with is customary canticles; since we read, that our holy forefathers promptly fulfilled in one day what we lukewarm monks should, please God, perform at least in a week.

CHAPTER XIX
Of the Manner of Reciting the Psalter

We believe that God is present everywhere and that the eyes of the Lord behold the good and the bad in every place (cf Prov 15:3). Let us firmly believe this, especially when we take part in the Work of God. Let us, therefore, always be mindful of what the Prophet saith, "Serve ye the Lord with fear" (Ps 2:11). And again, "Sing ye wisely" (Ps 46[47]:8). And, "I will sing praise to Thee in the sight of the angels" (Ps137[138]:1). Therefore, let us consider how it becometh us to behave in the sight of God and His angels, and let us so stand to sing, that our mind may be in harmony with our voice.

CHAPTER XX
Of Reverence at Prayer

If we do not venture to approach men who are in power, except with humility and reverence, when we wish to ask a favor, how much must we beseech the Lord God of all things with all humility and purity of devotion? And let us be assured that it is not in many words, but in the purity of heart and tears of compunction that we are heard. For this reason prayer ought to be short and pure, unless, perhaps it is lengthened by the inspiration of divine grace. At the community exercises, however, let the prayer always be short, and the sign having been given by the Superior, let all rise together.

CHAPTER XXI
Of the Deans of the Monastery

If the brotherhood is large, let brethren of good repute and holy life be chosen from among them and be appointed Deans; and let them take care of their deaneries in everything according to the commandments of God and the directions of their Abbot. Let such be chosen Deans as the Abbot may safely trust to share his burden.

Let them not be chosen for their rank, but for the merit of their life and their wisdom and knowledge; and if any of them, puffed up with pride, should be found blameworthy and, after having been corrected once and again and even a third time, refuseth to amend, let him be deposed, and one who is worthy be placed in his stead. We make the same regulation with reference to the Prior.

CHAPTER XXII
How the Monks Are to Sleep

Let the brethren sleep singly, each in a separate bed. Let them receive the bedding befitting their mode of life, according to the direction of their Abbot. If it can be done, let all sleep in one apartment; but if the number doth not allow it, let them sleep in tens or twenties with the seniors who have charge of them.

Let a light be kept burning constantly in the cell till morning. Let them sleep clothed and girded with cinctures or cords, that they may be always ready; but let them not have knives at their sides whilst they sleep, lest perchance the sleeping be wounded in their dreams; and the sign having been given, rising without delay, let them hasten to outstrip each other to the Work of God, yet with all gravity and decorum. Let the younger brethren not have their beds beside each other, but intermingled with the older ones; and rising to the Work of God, let them gently encourage one another on account of the excuses of the drowsy.

CHAPTER XXIII
Of Excommunication for Faults

If a brother is found stubborn or disobedient or proud or murmuring, or opposed to anything in the Holy Rule and a contemner of the commandments of his Superiors, let him be admonished by his Superiors once and again in secret, according to the command of our Lord (cf Mt 18:15-16). If he doth not amend let him be taken to task publicly before all. But if he doth not reform even then, and he understandeth what a penalty it is, let him be placed under excommunication; but if even then he remaineth obstinate let him undergo corporal punishment.

CHAPTER XXIV
What the Manner of Excommunication Should Be

The degree of excommunication or punishment ought to be meted out according to the gravity of the offense, and to determine that is left to the judgment of the Abbot. If, however, anyone of the brethren is detected in smaller faults, let him be debarred from eating at the common table.

The following shall be the practice respecting one who is excluded from the common table: that he does not intone a psalm or an antiphon nor read a lesson in the oratory until he hath made satisfaction; let him take his meal alone, after the refection of the brethren; thus: if, for instance, the brethren take their meal at the sixth hour that brother will take his at the ninth, and if the brethren take theirs at the ninth, he will take his in the evening, until by due satisfaction he obtaineth pardon.

CHAPTER XXV
Of Graver Faults

But let the brother who is found guilty of a graver fault be excluded from both the table and the oratory. Let none of the brethren join his company or speak with him. Let him be alone at the work enjoined on him, persevering in penitential sorrow, mindful of the terrible sentence of the Apostle who saith, that "such a man is delivered over for the destruction of the flesh, that the spirit may be saved in the day of the Lord" (1 Cor 5:5). Let him get his food alone in such quantity and at such a time as the Abbot shall deem fit; and let him not be blessed by anyone passing by, nor the food that is given him.

CHAPTER XXVI
Of Those Who without the Command of the Abbot Associate with the Excommunicated

If any brother presume to associate with an excommunicated brother in any way, or to speak with him, or to send him a message, without the command of the Abbot, let him incur the same penalty of excommunication.

CHAPTER XXVII
How Concerned the Abbot Should Be about the Excommunicated

Let the Abbot show all care and concern towards offending brethren because "they that are in health need not a physician, but they that are sick" (Mt 9:12). Therefore, like a prudent physician he ought to use every opportunity to send consolers, namely, discreet elderly brethren, to console the wavering brother, as it were, in secret, and induce him to make humble satisfaction; and let them cheer him up "lest he be swallowed up with overmuch sorrow" (2 Cor 2:7); but, as the same Apostle saith, "confirm your charity towards him" (2 Cor 2:8); and let prayer be said for him by all. The Abbot must take the utmost pains, and strive with all prudence and zeal, that none of the flock entrusted to him perish. For the Abbot must know that he has taken upon himself the care of infirm souls, not a despotism over the strong; and let him fear the threat of the Prophet wherein the Lord saith: "What ye saw to be fat, that ye took to yourselves, and what was diseased you threw away" (Ezek 34:3-4). And let him follow the loving example of the Good Shepherd, who, leaving the ninety-nine sheep on the mountains, went to seek the one that had gone astray, on whose weakness He had such pity, that He was pleased to lay it on His sacred shoulders and thus carry it back to the fold (cf Lk 15:5).

CHAPTER XXVIII
Of Those Who Having Often Been Corrected Do Not Amend

If a brother hath often been corrected and hath even been excommunicated for a fault and doth not amend, let a more severe correction be applied to him, namely, proceed against him with corporal punishment.

But if even then he doth not reform, or puffed up with pride, should perhaps, which God forbid, even defend his actions, then let the Abbot act like a prudent physician. After he hath applied soothing lotions, ointments of admonitions, medicaments of the Holy Scriptures, and if, as a last resource, he hath employed the caustic of excommunication and the blows of the lash, and seeth that even then his pains are of no avail, let him apply for that brother also what is more potent than all these measures: his own prayer and that of the brethren, that the Lord who is all-powerful may work a cure in that brother. But if he is not healed even in this way, then finally let the Abbot dismiss him from the community, as the Apostle saith: "Put away the evil one from among you" (1 Cor 5:13); and again: "If the faithless depart, let him depart" (1 Cor 7:15); lest one diseased sheep infect the whole flock.

CHAPTER XXIX
Whether Brethren Who Leave the Monastery Ought to Be Received Again

If a brother, who through his own fault leaveth the monastery or is expelled, desireth to return, let him first promise full amendment of the fault for which he left; and thus let him be received in the last place, that by this means his humility may be tried. If he should leave again, let him be received even a third time, knowing that after this every means of return will be denied him.

CHAPTER XXX
How Young Boys Are to Be Corrected

Every age and understanding should have its proper discipline. Whenever, therefore, boys or immature youths or such as can not understand how grave a penalty excommunication is, are guilty of a serious fault, let them undergo severe fasting or be disciplined with corporal punishment, that they may be corrected.

CHAPTER XXXI
The Kind of Man the Cellarer of the Monastery Ought to Be

Let there be chosen from the brotherhood as Cellarer of the monastery a wise man, of settled habits, temperate and frugal, not conceited, irritable, resentful, sluggish, or wasteful, but fearing God, who may be as a father to the whole brotherhood.

Let him have the charge of everything, let him do nothing without the command of the Abbot, let him do what hath been ordered him and not grieve the brethren. If a brother should perchance request anything of him unreasonably let him not sadden the brother with a cold refusal, but politely and with humility refuse him who asketh amiss. Let him be watchful of his own soul, always mindful of the saying of the Apostle: "For they that have ministered well, shall purchase to themselves a good degree" (1 Tm 3:13). Let him provide for the sick, the children, the guests, and the poor, with all care, knowing that, without doubt, he will have to give an account of all these things on judgment day. Let him regard all the vessels of the monastery and all its substance, as if they were sacred vessels of the altar. Let him neglect nothing and let him not give way to avarice, nor let him be wasteful and a squanderer of the goods of the monastery; but let him do all things in due measure and according to the bidding of his Abbot.

Above all things, let him be humble; and if he hath not the things to give, let him answer with a kind word, because it is written: "A good word is above the best gift" (Sir 18:17). Let him have under his charge everything that the Abbot hath entrusted to him, and not presume to meddle with matters forbidden him. Let him give the brethren their apportioned allowance without a ruffle or delay, that they may not be scandalized, mindful of what the Divine Word declareth that he deserveth who shall scandalize one of these little ones: "It were better for him that a millstone were hanged about his neck and that he were drowned in the depth of the sea" (Mt 18:6).

If the community is large, let assistants be given him, that, with their help, he too may fulfil the office entrusted to him with an even temper. Let the things that are to be given be distributed, and the things that are to be gotten asked for at the proper times, so that nobody may be disturbed or grieved in the house of God.

CHAPTER XXXII
Of the Tools and Goods of the Monastery

Let the Abbot appoint brethren on whose life and character he can rely, over the property of the monastery in tools, clothing, and things generally, and let him assign to them, as he shall deem proper, all the articles which must be collected after use and stored away.

Let the Abbot keep a list of these articles, so that, when the brethren in turn succeed each other in these trusts, he may know what he giveth and what he receiveth back. If anyone, however, handleth the goods of the monastery slovenly or carelessly let him be reprimanded and if he doth not amend let him come under the discipline of the Rule.

CHAPTER XXXIII
Whether Monks Ought to Have Anything of Their Own

The vice of personal ownership must by all means be cut out in the monastery by the very root, so that no one may presume to give or receive anything without the command of the Abbot; nor to have anything whatever as his own, neither a book, nor a writing tablet, nor a pen, nor anything else whatsoever, since monks are allowed to have neither their bodies nor their wills in their own power. Everything that is necessary, however, they must look for from the Father of the monastery; and let it not be allowed for anyone to have anything which the Abbot did not give or permit him to have. Let all things be common to all, as it is written. And let no one call or take to himself anything as his own (cf Acts 4:32). But if anyone should be found to indulge this most baneful vice, and, having been admonished once and again, doth not amend, let him be subjected to punishment.

CHAPTER XXXIV
Whether All Should Receive in Equal Measure What Is Necessary

It is written, "Distribution was made to everyone according as he had need" (Acts 4:35). We do not say by this that respect should be had for persons (God forbid), but regard for infirmities. Let him who hath need of less thank God and not give way to sadness, but let him who hath need of more, humble himself for his infirmity, and not be elated for the indulgence shown him; and thus all the members will be at peace.

Above all, let not the evil of murmuring appear in the least word or sign for any reason whatever. If anyone be found guilty herein, let him be placed under very severe discipline.

CHAPTER XXXV
Of the Weekly Servers in the Kitchen

Let the brethren serve each other so that no one be excused from the work in the kitchen, except on account of sickness or more necessary work, because greater merit and more charity is thereby acquired. Let help be given to the weak, however, that they may not do this work with sadness; but let all have help according to the size of the community and the circumstances of the place. If the community is large, let the Cellarer be excused from the kitchen, or if, as we have said, any are engaged in more urgent work; let the rest serve each other in charity.

Let him who is to go out of the weekly service, do the cleaning on Saturday. Let him wash the towels with which the brethren wipe their hands and feet. Let him who goeth out, as well as him who is to come in, wash the feet of all. Let him return the utensils of his department to the Cellarer clean and whole. Let the Cellarer give the same to the one who cometh in, so that he may know what he giveth and what he receiveth back.

An hour before meal time let the weekly servers receive each a cup of drink and a piece of bread over the prescribed portion, that they may serve their brethren at the time time of refection without murmuring and undue strain. On solemn feast days, however, let them abstain till after Mass.

As soon as the morning office on Sunday is ended, let the weekly servers who come in and who go out, cast themselves upon their knees in the oratory before all, asking their prayers. Let him who goeth out of the weekly service, say the following verse: Benedictus es, Domine Deus, qui adjuvisti me et consolatus se me (Dan 3:52; Ps 85[86]:17). The one going out having said this three times and received the blessing, let the one who cometh in follow and say: Deus in adjutorium meum intende; Domine, ad adjuvandum me festina (Ps 69[70]:2). And let this also be repeated three times by all, and having received the blessing let him enter upon his weekly service.

CHAPTER XXXVI
Of the Sick Brethren

Before and above all things, care must be taken of the sick, that they be served in very truth as Christ is served; because He hath said, "I was sick and you visited Me" (Mt 25:36).

And "As long as you did it to one of these My least brethren, you did it to Me" (Mt 25:40). But let the sick themselves also consider that they are served for the honor of God, and let them not grieve their brethren who serve them by unnecessary demands. These must, however, be patiently borne with, because from such as these a more bountiful reward is gained. Let the Abbot's greatest concern, therefore, be that they suffer no neglect.

Let a cell be set apart for the sick brethren, and a God-fearing, diligent, and careful attendant be appointed to serve them. Let the use of the bath be offered to the sick as often as it is useful, but let it be granted more rarely to the healthy and especially the young.

Thus also let the use of meat be granted to the sick and to the very weak for their recovery. But when they have been restored let them all abstain from meat in the usual manner.

But let the Abbot exercise the utmost care that the sick are not neglected by the Cellarer or the attendants, because whatever his disciples do amiss falleth back on him.

CHAPTER XXXVII
Of the Aged and Children

Although human nature is of itself drawn to feel compassion for these life-periods, namely, old age and childhood, still, let the decree of the Rule make provision also for them. Let their natural weakness be always taken into account and let the strictness of the Rule not be kept with them in respect to food, but let there be a tender regard in their behalf and let them eat before regular hours.

CHAPTER XXXVIII
Of the Weekly Reader

Reading must not be wanting at the table of the brethren when they are eating. Neither let anyone who may chance to take up the book venture to read there; but let him who is to read for the whole week enter upon that office on Sunday. After Mass and Communion let him ask all to pray for him that God may ward off from him the spirit of pride. And let the following verse be said three times by all in the oratory, he beginning it: Domine, labia mea aperies, et os meum annuntiabit laudem tuam (Ps 50[51]:17), and thus having received the blessing let him enter upon the reading.

Let the deepest silence be maintained that no whispering or voice be heard except that of the reader alone. But let the brethren so help each other to what is needed for eating and drinking, that no one need ask for anything. If, however, anything should be wanted, let it be asked for by means of a sign of any kind rather than a sound. And let no one presume to ask any questions there, either about the book or anything else, in order that no cause to speak be given [to the devil] (Eph 4:27; 1 Tm 5:14), unless, perchance, the Superior wisheth to say a few words for edification.

Let the brother who is reader for the week take a little bread and wine before he beginneth to read, on account of Holy Communion, and lest it should be too hard for him to fast so long. Afterward, however, let him take his meal in the kitchen with the weekly servers and the waiters. The brethren, however, will not read or sing in order, but only those who edify their hearers.

CHAPTER XXXIX
Of the Quantity of Food

Making allowance for the infirmities of different persons, we believe that for the daily meal, both at the sixth and the ninth hour, two kinds of cooked food are sufficient at all meals; so that he who perchance cannot eat of one, may make his meal of the other. Let two kinds of cooked food, therefore, be sufficient for all the brethren. And if there be fruit or fresh vegetables, a third may be added.

Let a pound of bread be sufficient for the day, whether there be only one meal or both dinner and supper.

If they are to eat supper, let a third part of the pound be reserved by the Cellarer and be given at supper.

If, however, the work hath been especially hard, it is left to the discretion and power of the Abbot to add something, if he think fit, barring above all things every excess, that a monk be not overtaken by indigestion. For nothing is so contrary to Christians as excess, as our Lord saith: "See that your hearts be not overcharged with surfeiting" (Lk 21:34).

Let the same quantity of food, however, not be served out to young children but less than to older ones, observing measure in all things.

But let all except the very weak and the sick abstain altogether from eating the flesh of four-footed animals.

CHAPTER XL
Of the Quantity of Drink

"Every one hath his proper gift from God, one after this manner and another after that" (1 Cor 7:7). It is with some hesitation, therefore, that we determine the measure of nourishment for others. However, making allowance for the weakness of the infirm, we think one hemina of wine a day is sufficient for each one. But to whom God granteth the endurance of abstinence, let them know that they will have their special reward. If the circumstances of the place, or the work, or the summer's heat should require more, let that depend on the judgment of the Superior, who must above all things see to it, that excess or drunkenness do not creep in.

Although we read that wine is not at all proper for monks, yet, because monks in our times cannot be persuaded of this, let us agree to this, at least, that we do not drink to satiety, but sparingly; because "wine maketh even wise men fall off" (Sir 19:2). But where the poverty of the place will not permit the aforesaid measure to be had, but much less, or none at all, let those who live there bless God and murmur not. This we charge above all things, that they live without murmuring.

CHAPTER XLI
At What Times the Brethren Should Take Their Refection

From holy Easter till Pentecost let the brethren dine at the sixth hour and take supper in the evening. From Pentecost on, however, during the whole summer, if the monks have no work in the fields and the excess of the heat doth not interfere, let them fast on Wednesday and Friday until the ninth hour; but on the other days let them dine at the sixth hour. This sixth hour for dinner is to be continued, if they have work in the fields or the heat of the summer is great. Let the Abbot provide for this; and so let him manage and adapt everything that souls may be saved, and that what the brethren do, they may do without having a reasonable cause to murmur.

From the ides of September until the beginning of Lent let them always dine at the ninth hour. During Lent, however, until Easter, let them dine in the evening. But let this evening hour be so arranged that they will not need lamp-light during their meal; but let everything be finished whilst it is still day. But at all times let the hour of meals, whether for dinner or for supper, be so arranged that everything is done by daylight.

CHAPTER XLII
That No One Speak after Complin

Monks should always be given to silence, especially, however, during the hours of the night. Therefore, on every day, whether of fast or of a mid-day meal, as soon as they have risen from their evening meal, let all sit together in one place, and let one read the Conferences or the Lives of the Fathers, or something else that will edify the hearers; not, however, the Heptateuch or the Books of the Kings, because it would not be wholesome for weak minds to hear this part of the Scripture at that hour; they should, however, be read at other times. But if it was a fast-day, then, when Vespers have been said, and after a short interval, let them next come together for the reading of the Conferences, as we have said; and when the four or five pages have been read, or as much as the hour will permit, and all have assembled in one place during the time of the reading, let him also come who was perchance engaged in work enjoined on him. All, therefore, having assembled in one place, let them say Complin, and after going out from Complin, let there be no more permission from that time on for anyone to say anything. If, however, anyone is found to break this rule, let him undergo heavy punishment, unless the needs of guests should arise, or the Abbot should perhaps give a command to anyone. But let even this be done with the utmost gravity and moderation.

CHAPTER XLIII
Of Those Who Are Tardy in Coming to the Work of God or to Table

As soon as the signal for the time of the divine office is heard, let everyone, leaving whatever he hath in his hands, hasten with all speed, yet with gravity, that there may be no cause for levity. Therefore, let nothing be preferred to the Work of God. If at Matins anyone cometh after the Gloria of the 94th psalm, which on that account we wish to be much drawn out and said slowly, let him not stand in his place in the choir; but let him stand last of all, or in a place which the Abbot hath set apart for such careless ones, that he may be seen by him and by all, until, the Work of God being ended, he maketh satisfaction by public penance. The reason, however, why we think they should stand in the last place, or apart from the rest, is this, that seen by all they may amend for very shame. For if they stayed outside the oratory, there might be one who would go back to sleep, or anyhow would seat himself outside, indulge in vain gossip, and give a "chance to the devil" (Eph 4:27; 1 Tm 5:14). Let him go inside, therefore, that he may not lose the whole, and may amend for the future.

At the day hours, however, whoever doth not arrive for the Work of God after the verse and the Gloria of the first psalm, which is said after the verse, let him stand in the last place, according to the rule which we stated above; and let him not attempt to join the choir of the chanters until he hath made satisfaction, unless, perchance, the Abbot's permission hath given him leave to do so, with the understanding that he atone the fault afterwards.

If anyone doth not come to table before the verse, so that all may say the verse and pray together and sit down to table at the same time, let him be twice corrected for this, if he failed to come through his own fault and negligence. If he doth not amend after this, let him not be permitted to eat at the common table; but separated from the company of all, let him eat alone, his portion of wine being taken from him, until he hath made satisfaction and hath amended. In like manner let him suffer who is not present also at the verse which is said after the refection.

And let no one presume to take food or drink before or after the appointed time. But if anything should be offered to a brother by the Superior and he refuseth to accept it, and afterwards desireth what at first he refused or anything else, let him receive nothing at all, until he maketh due satisfaction.

CHAPTER XLIV
Of Those Who Are Excommunicated—How They Make Satisfaction

Whoever is excommunicated for graver faults from the oratory and the table, let him, at the time that the Work of God is celebrated in the oratory, lie stretched, face down in silence before the door of the oratory at the feet of all who pass out. And let him do this until the Abbot judgeth that it is enough. When he then cometh at the Abbot's bidding, let him cast himself at the Abbot's feet, then at the feet of all, that they may pray for him. If then the Abbot ordereth it, let him be received back into the choir in the place which the Abbot shall direct; yet so that he doth not presume to intone a psalm or a lesson or anything else in the oratory, unless the Abbot again biddeth him to do so. Then, at all the Hours, when the Work of God is ended, let him cast himself on the ground in the place where he standeth, and thus let him make satisfaction, until the Abbot again biddeth him finally to cease from this penance.

But let those who are excommunicated for lighter faults from the table only make satisfaction in the oratory, as long as the Abbot commandeth, and let them perform this until he giveth his blessing and saith, "It is enough."

CHAPTER XLV
Of Those Who Commit a Fault in the Oratory

If anyone whilst he reciteth a psalm, a responsory, an antiphon, or a lesson, maketh a mistake, and doth not humble himself there before all by making satisfaction, let him undergo a greater punishment, because he would not correct by humility what he did amiss through negligence. But let children be beaten for such a fault.

CHAPTER XLVI
Of Those Who Fail in Any Other Matters

If anyone whilst engaged in any work, in the kitchen, in the cellar, in serving, in the bakery, in the garden, at any art or work in any place whatever, committeth a fault, or breaketh or loseth anything, or transgresseth in any way whatever, and he doth not forthwith come before the Abbot and the community, and of his own accord confess his offense and make satisfaction, and it becometh known through another, let him be subjected to a greater correction.

If, however, the cause of the offense is secret, let him disclose it to the Abbot alone, or to his spiritual Superiors, who know how to heal their own wounds, and not expose and make public those of others.

CHAPTER XLVII
Of Giving the Signal for the Time of the Work of God

Let it be the Abbot's care that the time for the Work of God be announced both by day and by night; either to announce it himself, or to entrust this charge to a careful brother that everything may be done at the proper time.

Let those who have been ordered, intone the psalms or the antiphons in their turn after the Abbot. No one, however, should presume to sing or read unless he is able so to perform this office that the hearers may be edified; and let it be done with humility, gravity, and reverence by him whom the Abbot hath ordered.

CHAPTER XLVIII
Of the Daily Work

Idleness is the enemy of the soul; and therefore the brethren ought to be employed in manual labor at certain times, at others, in devout reading. Hence, we believe that the time for each will be properly ordered by the following arrangement; namely, that from Easter till the calends of October, they go out in the morning from the first till about the fourth hour, to do the necessary work, but that from the fourth till about the sixth hour they devote to reading. After the sixth hour, however, when they have risen from table, let them rest in their beds in complete silence; or if, perhaps, anyone desireth to read for himself, let him so read that he doth not disturb others. Let None be said somewhat earlier, about the middle of the eighth hour; and then let them work again at what is necessary until Vespers.

If, however, the needs of the place, or poverty should require that they do the work of gathering the harvest themselves, let them not be downcast, for then are they monks in truth, if they live by the work of their hands, as did also our forefathers and the Apostles.

However, on account of the faint-hearted let all things be done with moderation.

From the calends of October till the beginning of Lent, let them apply themselves to reading until the second hour complete. At the second hour let Tierce be said, and then let all be employed in the work which hath been assigned to them till the ninth hour. When, however, the first signal for the hour of None hath been given, let each one leave off from work and be ready when the second signal shall strike.

But after their repast let them devote themselves to reading or the psalms.

During the Lenten season let them be employed in reading from morning until the third hour, and till the tenth hour let them do the work which is imposed on them. During these days of Lent let all received books from the library, and let them read them through in order. These books are to be given out at the beginning of the Lenten season.

Above all, let one or two of the seniors be appointed to go about the monastery during the time that the brethren devote to reading and take notice, lest perhaps a slothful brother be found who giveth himself up to idleness or vain talk, and doth not attend to his reading, and is unprofitable, not only to himself, but disturbeth also others.

If such a one be found (which God forbid), let him be punished once and again. If he doth not amend, let him come under the correction of the Rule in such a way that others may fear. And let not brother join brother at undue times. On Sunday also let all devote themselves to reading, except those who are appointed to the various functions. But if anyone should be so careless and slothful that he will not or cannot meditate or read, let some work be given him to do, that he may not be idle.

Let such work or charge be given to the weak and the sickly brethren, that they are neither idle, nor so wearied with the strain of work that they are driven away. Their weakness must be taken into account by the Abbot.

CHAPTER XLIX
On the Keeping of Lent

The life of a monk ought always to be a Lenten observance. However, since such virtue is that of few, we advise that during these days of Lent he guard his life with all purity and at the same time wash away during these holy days all the shortcomings of other times. This will then be worthily done, if we restrain ourselves from all vices.

Let us devote ourselves to tearful prayers, to reading and compunction of heart, and to abstinence.

During these days, therefore, let us add something to the usual amount of our service, special prayers, abstinence from food and drink, that each one offer to God "with the joy of the Holy Ghost" (1 Thes 1:6), of his own accord, something above his prescribed measure; namely, let him withdraw from his body somewhat of food, drink, sleep, speech, merriment, and with the gladness of spiritual desire await holy Easter.

Let each one, however, make known to his Abbot what he offereth and let it be done with his approval and blessing; because what is done without permission of the spiritual father will be imputed to presumption and vain glory, and not to merit. Therefore, let all be done with the approval of the Abbot.

CHAPTER L
Of Brethren Who Work a Long Distance from the Oratory or Are on a Journey

The brethren who are at work too far away, and cannot come to the oratory at the appointed time, and the Abbot hath assured himself that such is the case—let them perform the Work of God in the fear of God and on bended knees where they are working.

In like manner let those who are sent on a journey not permit the appointed hours to pass by; but let them say the office by themselves as best they can, and not neglect to fulfil the obligation of divine service.

CHAPTER LI
Of the Brethren Who Do Not Go Very Far Away

A brother who is sent out on any business and is expected to return to the monastery the same day, may not presume to eat outside, even though he be urgently requested to do so, unless, indeed, it is commanded him by his Abbot. If he act otherwise, let him be excommunicated.

CHAPTER LII
Of the Oratory of the Monastery

Let the oratory be what it is called, and let nothing else be done or stored there. When the Work of God is finished, let all go out with the deepest silence, and let reverence be shown to God; that a brother who perhaps desireth to pray especially by himself is not prevented by another's misconduct. But if perhaps another desireth to pray alone in private, let him enter with simplicity and pray, not with a loud voice, but with tears and fervor of heart. Therefore, let him who doth not say his prayers in this way, not be permitted to stay in the oratory after the Work of God is finished, as we said, that another may not be disturbed.

CHAPTER LIII
Of the Reception of Guests

Let all guests who arrive be received as Christ, because He will say: "I was a stranger and you took Me in" (Mt 25:35). And let due honor be shown to all, especially to those "of the household of the faith" (Gal 6:10) and to wayfarers.

When, therefore, a guest is announced, let him be met by the Superior and the brethren with every mark of charity. And let them first pray together, and then let them associate with one another in peace.

This kiss of peace should not be given before a prayer hath first been said, on account of satanic deception. In the greeting let all humility be shown to the guests, whether coming or going; with the head bowed down or the whole body prostrate on the ground, let Christ be adored in them as He is also received.

When the guests have been received, let them be accompanied to prayer, and after that let the Superior, or whom he shall bid, sit down with them. Let the divine law be read to the guest that he may be edified, after which let every kindness be shown him. Let the fast be broken by the Superior in deference to the guest, unless, perchance, it be a day of solemn fast, which cannot be broken. Let the brethren, however, keep the customary fast. Let the Abbot pour the water on the guest's hands, and let both the Abbot and the whole brotherhood wash the feet of all the guests. When they have been washed, let them say this verse: "We have received Thy mercy, O God, in the midst of Thy temple" (Ps 47[48]:10). Let the greatest care be taken, especially in the reception of the poor and travelers, because Christ is received more specially in them; whereas regard for the wealthy itself procureth them respect.

Let the kitchen of the Abbot and the guests be apart, that the brethren may not be disturbed by the guests who arrive at uncertain times and who are never wanting in the monastery. Let two brothers who are able to fulfil this office well go into the kitchen for a year. Let help be given them as they need it, that they may serve without murmuring; and when they have not enough to do, let them go out again for work where it is commanded them.

Let this course be followed, not only in this office, but in all the offices of the monastery—that whenever the brethren need help, it be given them, and that when they have nothing to do, they again obey orders. Moreover, let also a God-fearing brother have assigned to him the apartment of the guests, where there should be sufficient number of beds made up; and let the house of God be wisely managed by the wise. On no account let anyone who is not ordered to do so, associate or speak with guests; but if he meet or see them, having saluted them humbly, as we have said, and asked a blessing, let him pass on saying that he is not allowed to speak with a guest.

CHAPTER LIV
Whether a Monk Should Receive Letters or Anything Else

Let it not be allowed at all for a monk to give or to receive letters, tokens, or gifts of any kind, either from parents or any other person, nor from each other, without the permission of the Abbot. But even if anything is sent him by his parents, let him not presume to accept it before it hath been make known to the Abbot. And if he order it to be accepted, let it be in the Abbot's power to give it to whom he pleaseth. And let not the brother to whom perchance it was sent, become sad, that "no chance be given to the devil" (Eph 4:27; 1 Tm 5:14). But whosoever shall presume to act otherwise, let him fall under the discipline of the Rule.

CHAPTER LV
Of the Clothing and the Footgear of the Brethren

Let clothing be given to the brethren according to the circumstances of the place and the nature of the climate in which they live, because in cold regions more in needed, while in warm regions less. This consideration, therefore, resteth with the Abbot. We believe, however, that for a temperate climate a cowl and a tunic for each monk are sufficient,—a woolen cowl for winter and a thin or worn one for summer, and a scapular for work, and stockings and shoes as covering for the feet. Let the monks not worry about the color or the texture of all these things, but let them be such as can be bought more cheaply.

Let the Abbot, however, look to the size, that these garments are not too small, but fitted for those who are to wear them.

Let those who receive new clothes always return the old ones, to be put away in the wardrobe for the poor. For it is sufficient for a monk to have two tunics and two cowls, for wearing at night and for washing. Hence, what is over and above is superfluous and must be taken away. So, too, let them return stockings and whatever is old, when they receive anything new. Let those who are sent out on a journey receive trousers from the wardrobe, which, on their return, they will replace there, washed. The cowls and the tunics should also be a little better than the ones they usually wear, which they received from the wardrobe when they set out on a journey, and give back when they return.

For their bedding, let a straw mattress, a blanket, a coverlet, and a pillow be sufficient. These beds must, however, be frequently examined by the Abbot, to prevent personal goods from being found. And if anything should be found with anyone that he did not receive from the Abbot, let him fall under the severest discipline. And that this vice of private ownership may be cut off by the root, let everything necessary be given by the Abbot; namely, cowl, tunic, stockings, shoes, girdle, knife, pen, needle, towel, writing tablet; that all pretence of want may be removed. In this connection, however, let the following sentence from the Acts of the Apostles always be kept in mind by the Abbot: "And distribution was made to every man according as he had need" (Acts 4:35). In this manner, therefore, let the Abbot also have regard for the infirmities of the needy, not for the bad will of the envious. Yet in all his decisions, let the Abbot think of God's retribution.

CHAPTER LVI
Of the Abbot's Table

Let the Abbot's table always be with the guests and travelers. When, however, there are no guests, let it be in his power to invite any of the brethren he desireth. Let him provide, however, that one or two of the seniors always remain with the brethren for the sake of discipline.

CHAPTER LVII
Of the Artists of the Monastery

If there be skilled workmen in the monastery, let them work at their art in all humility, if the Abbot giveth his permission. But if anyone of them should grow proud by reason of his art, in that he seemeth to confer a benefit on the monastery, let him be removed from that work and not return to it, unless after he hath humbled himself, the Abbot again ordereth him to do so. But if any of the work of the artists is to be sold, let them, through whose hands the transaction must pass, see to it, that they do not presume to practice any fraud on the monastery.

Let them always be mindful of Ananias and Saphira, lest, perhaps, the death which these suffered in the body (cf Acts 5:1-11), they and all who practice any fraud in things belonging to the monastery suffer in the soul. On the other hand, as regards the prices of these things, let not the vice of avarice creep in, but let it always be given a little cheaper than it can be given by seculars, That God May Be Glorified in All Things (1 Pt 4:11).

CHAPTER LVIII
Of the Manner of Admitting Brethren

Let easy admission not be given to one who newly cometh to change his life; but, as the Apostle saith, "Try the spirits, whether they be of God" (1 Jn 4:1). If, therefore, the newcomer keepeth on knocking, and after four or five days it is seen that he patiently beareth the harsh treatment offered him and the difficulty of admission, and that he persevereth in his request, let admission be granted him, and let him live for a few days in the apartment of the guests.

But afterward let him live in the apartment of novices, and there let him meditate, eat, and sleep. Let a senior also be appointed for him, who is qualified to win souls, who will observe him with great care and see whether he really seeketh God, whether he is eager for the Work of God, obedience and humiliations. Let him be shown all the hard and rugged things through which we pass on to God.

If he promiseth to remain steadfast, let this Rule be read to him in order after the lapse of two months, and let it be said to him: Behold the law under which thou desirest to combat. If thou canst keep it, enter; if, however, thou canst not, depart freely. If he still persevereth, then let him be taken back to the aforesaid apartment of the novices, and let him be tried again in all patience. And after the lapse of six months let the Rule be read over to him, that he may know for what purpose he entereth. And if he still remaineth firm, let the same Rule be read to him again after four months. And if, after having weighed the matter with himself he promiseth to keep everything, and to do everything that is commanded him, then let him be received into the community, knowing that he is now placed under the law of the Rule, and that from that day forward it is no longer permitted to him to wrest his neck from under the yoke of the Rule, which after so long a deliberation he was at liberty either to refuse or to accept.

Let him who is received promise in the oratory, in the presence of all, before God and His saints, stability, the conversion of morals, and obedience, in order that, if he should ever do otherwise, he may know that he will be condemned by God "Whom he mocketh." Let him make a written statement of his promise in the name of the saints whose relics are there, and of the Abbot there present. Let him write this document with his own hand; or at least, if he doth not know how to write, let another write it at his request, and let the novice make his mark, and with his own hand place it on the altar. When he hath placed it there, let the novice next begin the verse: "Uphold me, O Lord, according to Thy word and I shall live; and let me not be confounded in my expectations" (Ps 118[119]:116).

Then let all the brotherhood repeat this verse three times, adding the Gloria Patri. The let that novice brother cast himself down at the feet of all, that they may pray for him; and from that day let him be counted in the brotherhood. If he hath any property, let him first either dispose of it to the poor or bestow it on the monastery by a formal donation, reserving nothing for himself as indeed he should know that from that day onward he will no longer have power even over his own body.

Let him, therefore, be divested at once in the oratory of the garments with which he is clothed, and be vested in the garb of the monastery. But let the clothes of which he was divested by laid by in the wardrobe to be preserved, that, if on the devil's suasion he should ever consent to leave the monastery (which God forbid) he be then stripped of his monastic habit and cast out. **But let him**

CHAPTER LIX
Of the Children of the Noble and of the Poor Who Are Offered

If it happen that a nobleman offereth his son to God in the monastery and the boy is of tender age, let his parents execute the written promise which we have mentioned above; and with the oblation let them wrap that document and the boy's hand in the altar cloth and thus offer him.

As to their property, let them bind themselves under oath in the same document that they will never give him anything themselves nor through any other person, nor in any way whatever, nor leave a chance for his owning anything; or else, if they refuse to do this and want to make an offering to the monastery as an alms for their own benefit, let them make a donation to the monastery ofwhatever goods they wish to give, reserving to themselves the income of it, if they so desire. And let everything be so barred that the boy remain in no uncertainty, which might deceive and ruin him (which God forbid)—a pass we have learned by experience.

Let those who are poor act in like manner. But as to those who have nothing at all, let them simply make the declaration, and with the oblation offer their son in the presence of witnesses.

CHAPTER LX
Of Priests Who May Wish to Live in the Monastery

If a priest asketh to be received into the monastery, let consent not be granted too readily; still, if he urgently persisteth in his request, let him know that he must keep the whole discipline of the Rule, and that nothing will be relaxed in his favor, that it may be as it is written: "Friend, whereunto art thou come" (Mt 26:25)?

It may be granted him, however, to stand next after the Abbot, and to give the blessing, or to celebrate Mass, but only if the Abbot ordereth him to do so; but if he doth not bid him, let him not presume to do anything under whatever consideration, knowing that he is under the discipline of the Rule, and let him rather give examples of humility to all. But if there is a question of an appointment in the monastery, or any other matter, let him be ranked by the time of his entry into the monastery, and not by the place granted him in consideration of the priesthood. But if a cleric, moved by the same desire, wisheth to join the monastery, let him too have a middle place, provided he promiseth to keep the Rule and personal stability.

CHAPTER LXI
How Stranger Monks Are to Be Received

If a monk who is a stranger, arriveth from a distant place and desireth to live in the monastery as a guest, and is satisfied with the customs he findeth there, and doth not trouble the monastery with superfluous wants, but is satisfied with what he findeth, let him be received for as long a time as he desireth. Still, if he should reasonably, with humility and charity, censure or point out anything, let the Abbot consider discreetly whether the Lord did not perhaps send him for that very purpose. If later on he desireth to declare his stability let his wish not be denied, and especially since his life could be known during his stay as a guest.

But if during the time that he was a guest he was found to be troublesome and disorderly, he must not only not associate with the monastic body but should even be politely requested to leave, that others may not be infected by his evil life. But if he hath not been such as deserveth to be cast forth, he should not only be admitted to join the brotherhood, if he apply, but he should even be urged to remain, that others may be taught by his example, because we serve one Lord and fight under one King everywhere. If the Abbot recognize him to be such a one he may also place him in a somewhat higher rank.

The Abbot may, however, place not only a monk, but also those of the aforesaid grades of priests and clerics, in a higher place than that of their entry, if he seeth their lives to be such as to deserve it. But let the Abbot take care never to admit a monk of any other known monastery to residence, without the consent of his Abbot or commendatory letters, because it is written: "What thou wilt not have done to thyself, do not to another" (Tb 4:16).

CHAPTER LXII
Of the Priests of the Monastery

If the Abbot desireth to have a priest or a deacon ordained, let him select from among his monks one who is worthy to discharge the priestly office.

But let the one who hath been ordained be on his guard against arrogance and pride, and let him not attempt to do anything but what is commanded him by the Abbot, knowing that he is now all the more subject to the discipline of the Rule; and in consequence of the priesthood let him not forget the obedience and discipline of the Rule, but advance more and more in godliness.

Let him, however, always keep the place which he had when he entered the monastery, except when he is engaged in sacred functions, unless the choice of the community and the wish of the Abbot have promoted him in acknowledgment of the merit of his life. Let him know, however, that he must observe the Rule prescribed by the Deans and the Superiors.

If he should otherwise, let him be judged, not as a priest, but as a rebel; and if after frequent warnings he doth not amend, and his guilt is clearly shown, let him be cast forth from the monastery, provided his obstinacy is such that he will neither submit nor obey the Rule.

CHAPTER LXIII
Of the Order in the Monastery

Let all keep their order in the monastery in such wise, that the time of their conversion and the merit of their life distinguish it, or as the Abbot hath directed. Let the Abbot not disorder the flock committed to him, nor by an arbitrary use of his power dispose of anything unjustly; but let him always bear in mind that he will have to give an account to God of all his judgments and works. Hence in the order that he hath established, or that the brethren had, let them approach for the kiss of peace, for Communion, intone the psalms, and stand in choir.

And in no place whatever let age determine the order or be a disadvantage; because Samuel and Daniel when mere boys judged the priests (cf 1 Sam. 3; Dan 13:44-62).

Excepting those, therefore, whom, as we have said, the Abbot from higher motives hath advanced, or, for certain reasons, hath lowered, let all the rest take their place as they are converted: thus, for instance, let him who came into the monastery at the second hour of the day, know that he is younger than he who came at the first hour, whatever his age or dignity may be. Children are to be kept under discipline at all times and by everyone. Therefore, let the younger honor their elders, and the older love the younger.

In naming each other let no one be allowed to address another by his simple name; but let the older style the younger brethren, brothers; let the younger, however, call their elders, fathers, by which is implied the reverence due to a father. But because the Abbot is believed to hold the place of Christ, let him be styled Lord and Abbot, not only by assumption on his part, but out of love and reverence for Christ. Let him think of this and so show himself, that he be worthy of such an honor. Wherever, then, the brethren meet each other, let the younger ask the blessing from the older; and when the older passeth by, let the younger rise and give him place to sit; and let the younger not presume to sit down with him unless his elder biddeth him to do so, that it may be done as it is written: "In honor preventing one another" (Rom 12:10). Let children and boys take their places in the oratory and at table with all due discipline; outdoors, however, or wherever they may be, let them be under custody and discipline until they reach the age of understanding.

CHAPTER LXIV
Of the Election of the Abbot

In the election of an Abbot let this always be observed as a rule, that he be placed in the position whom the whole community with one consent, in the fear of God, or even a small part, with sounder judgment, shall elect. But let him who is to be elected be chosen for the merit of his life and the wisdom of his doctrine, though he be the last in the community.

But even if the whole community should by mutual consent elect a man who agreeth to connive at their evil ways (which God forbid) and these irregularities in some come to the knowledge of the Bishop to whose diocese the place belongeth, or to neighboring Abbots, or Christian people, let them not permit the intrigue of the wicked to succeed, but let them appoint a worthy steward over the house of God, knowing that they shall receive a bountiful reward for this action, if they do it with a pure intention and godly zeal; whereas, on the other hand, they commit a sin if they neglect it.

But when the Abbot hath been elected let him bear in mind how great a burden he hath taken upon himself, and to whom he must give an account of his stewardship (cf Lk 16:2); and let him be convinced that it becometh him better to serve than to rule. He must, therefore, be versed in the divine law, that he may know whence "to bring forth new things and old" (Mt 13:52). Let him be chaste, sober, and merciful, and let him always exalt "mercy above judgment" (Jas 2:13), that he also may obtain mercy.

Let him hate vice, but love the brethren. And even in his corrections, let him act with prudence and not go to extremes, lest, while he aimeth to remove the rust too thoroughly, the vessel be broken. Let him always keep his own frailty in mind, and remember that "the bruised reed must not be broken" (Is 42:3). In this we are not saying that he should allow evils to take root, but that he cut them off with prudence and charity, as he shall see it is best for each one, as we have already said; and let him aim to be loved rather than feared.

Let him not be fussy or over anxious, exacting, or headstrong; let him not be jealous or suspicious, because he will never have rest. In all his commands, whether they refer to things spiritual or temporal, let him be cautious and considerate. Let him be discerning and temperate in the tasks which he enjoineth, recalling the discretion of holy Jacob who saith: "If I should cause my flocks to be overdriven, they would all die in one day" (Gen 33:13). Keeping in view these and other dictates of discretion, the mother of virtues, let him so temper everything that the strong may still have something to desire and the weak may not draw back. Above all, let him take heed that he keep this Rule in all its detail; that when he hath served well he may hear from the Lord what the good servant heard who gave his fellow-servants bread in season: "Amen, I say to you," He saith,"he shall set him over all his goods" (Mt 24:47).

CHAPTER LXV
Of the Prior of the Monastery

It often happeneth indeed, that grave scandals arise in monasteries out of the appointment of the Prior; since there are some who, puffed up with the wicked spirit of pride and thinking themselves to be second Abbots, set up a despotic rule, foster scandals, and excite quarrels in the community, and especially in those places where also the Prior is appointed by the same Bishop or the same Abbots who appointeth his Abbot. How foolish this is can easily be seen; because, from the very beginning of his appointment, matter for pride is furnished him, when his thoughts suggest to him that now he is exempt from the authority of the Abbot, because "thou too hast been appointed by those by whom the Abbot was appointed." From this source arise envy, discord, slander, quarrels, jealousy, and disorders. While the Abbot and the Prior are thus at variance with each other, it must follow that their souls are endangered by this discord and that those who are under them, as long as they humor the parties, go to ruin.

The fault of this evil resteth on the heads of those who were the authors of such disorders.

We foresee, therefore, that for the preservation of peace and charity it is best that the government of the monastery should depend on the will of the Abbot; and if it can be done, let the affairs of the monastery (as we have explained before) be attended to by deans, as the Abbot shall dispose; so that, the same office being shared by many, no one may become proud.

If, however, the place require it, or the brotherhood reasonably and with humility make the request, and the Abbot shall deem it advisable, let the Abbot himself appoint as Prior whomever, with the advice of God-fearing brethren, he shall select. But let the Prior reverently do what his Abbot hath enjoined on him, doing nothing against the will or the direction of the Abbot; for the higher he is placed above others, the more careful should he be to obey the precepts of the Rule.

If the Prior be found disorderly or blinded by vainglory, or hath been proved to be a contemner of the Holy Rule, let him be admonished up to the fourth time; if he doth not amend, let the correction of the regular discipline be applied to him. But if he doth not amend even then, let him be deposed from the office of priorship, and another who is worthy be appointed in his stead.

But if even afterward he be not quiet and submissive in the brotherhood, let him also be expelled from the monastery. Still, let the Abbot reflect that he must give an account to God for all his judgments, lest perhaps envy or jealousy should sear his conscience.

CHAPTER LXVI
Of the Porter of the Monastery

Let a wise old man be placed at the door of the monastery, one who knoweth how to take and give an answer, and whose mature age doth not permit him to stray about.

The porter should have a cell near the door, that they who come may always find one present from whom they may obtain an answer. As soon as anyone knocketh or a poor person calleth, let him answer, "Thanks be to God," or invoke a blessing, and with the meekness of the fear of God let him return an answer speedily in the fervor of charity. If the porter hath need of assistance, let him have a younger brother.

If it can be done, the monastery should be so situated that all the necessaries, such as water, the mill, the garden, are enclosed, and the various arts may be plied inside of the monastery, so that there may be no need for the monks to go about outside, because it is not good for their souls. But we desire that this Rule be read quite often in the community, that none of the brethren may excuse himself of ignorance.

CHAPTER LXVII
Of the Brethren Who Are Sent on a Journey

Let the brethren who are to be sent on a journey recommend themselves to the prayers of all the brotherhood and of the Abbot. And after the last prayer at the Work of God, let a commemoration always be made for the absent brethren.

On the day that the brethren return from the journey, let them lie prostrate on the floor of the oratory at all the Canonical Hours, when the Work of God is finished, and ask the prayers of all on account of failings, for fear that the sight of evil or the sound of frivolous speech should have surprised them on the way.

And let no one presume to relate to another what he hath seen or heard outside of the monastery, because it is most hurtful. But if anyone presume to do so, let him undergo the penalty of the Rule. In like manner let him be punished who shall presume to go beyond the enclosure of the monastery, or anywhere else, or to do anything, however little, without the order of the Abbot.

CHAPTER LXVIII
If a Brother Is Commanded to Do Impossible Things

If, perchance, any difficult or impossible tasks be enjoined on a brother, let him nevertheless receive the order of him who commandeth with all meekness and obedience. If, however, he see that the gravity of the task is altogether beyond his strength, let him quietly and seasonably submit the reasons for his inability to his Superior, without pride, protest, or dissent. If, however, after his explanation the Superior still insisteth on his command, let the younger be convinced that so it is good for him; and let him obey from love, relying on the help of God.

CHAPTER LXIX
That in the Monastery No One Presume to Defend Another

Care must be taken that on no occasion one monk try to defend another in the monastery, or to take his part, even though they be closely related by ties of blood. Let it not be attempted by the monks in any way; because such conduct may give rise to very grave scandal. If anyone overstep this rule, let him be severely punished.

CHAPTER LXX
That No One Presume to Strike Another

Let every occasion for presumption be avoided in the monastery. We decree that no one be permitted to excommunicate or to strike any one of his brethren, unless the Abbot hath given him the authority. But let those who transgress be taken to task in the presence of all, that the others may fear (cf 1 Tm 5:20). Let all, however, exercise diligent and watchful care over the discipline of children, until the age of fifteen; but even that, within due limits and with discretion. For if anyone should presume to chastise those of more advanced years, without the command of the Abbot, or should be unduly provoked with children, let him be subject to the discipline of the Rule; because it is written: "What thou dost not wish to be done to thee, do not thou to another" (Tb 4:16).

CHAPTER LXXI
That the Brethren Be Obedient to One Another

The brethren must render the service of obedience not only to the Abbot, but they must thus also obey one another, knowing that they shall go to God by this path of obedience. Hence, granted the command of the Abbot and of the Superiors who are appointed by him (to which we do not permit private commands to be preferred), in other respects let the younger brethren obey their elders with all charity and zeal.

But if anyone is found to be obstinate, let him be punished.

And if a brother be punished in any way by the Abbot or by any of his Superiors for even a slight reason or if he perceive that the temper of any of his Superiors is but slightly ruffled or excited against him in the least, let him without delay cast himself down on the ground at his feet making satisfaction, until the agitation is quieted by a blessing. If anyone scorn to do this, either let him undergo corporal punishment, or, if he be obstinate, let him be expelled from the monastery.

CHAPTER LXXII
Of the Virtuous Zeal Which the Monks Ought to Have

As there is a harsh and evil zeal which separateth from God and leadeth to hell, so there is a virtuous zeal which separateth from vice and leadeth to God and life everlasting.

Let the monks, therefore, practice this zeal with most ardent love; namely, that in honor they forerun one another (cf Rom 12:10). Let them bear their infirmities, whether of body or mind, with the utmost patience; let them vie with one another in obedience. Let no one follow what he thinketh useful to himself, but rather to another. Let them practice fraternal charity with a chaste love.

Let them fear God and love their Abbot with sincere and humble affection; let them prefer nothing whatever to Christ, and my He lead us all together to life everlasting.

CHAPTER LXXIII
Of This, that Not the Whole Observance of Righteousness Is Laid Down in this Rule

Now, we have written this Rule that, observing it in monasteries, we may show that we have acquired at least some moral righteousness, or a beginning of the monastic life.

On the other hand, he that hasteneth on to the perfection of the religious life, hath at hand the teachings of the holy Fathers, the observance of which leadeth a man to the height of perfection. For what page or what utterance of the divinely inspired books of the Old and the New Testament is not a most exact rule of human life? Or, what book of the holy Catholic Fathers doth not loudly proclaim how we may go straight to our Creator? So, too, the collations of the Fathers, and their institutes and lives, and the rule of our holy Father, Basil—what are they but the monuments of the virtues of exemplary and obedient monks? But for us slothful, disedifying, and negligent monks they are a source for shame and confusion.

Thou, therefore, who hastenest to the heavenly home, with the help of Christ fulfil this least rule written for a beginning; and then thou shalt with God's help attain at last to the greater heights of knowledge and virtue which we have mentioned above.

For more wonderful
Traditional Catholic Books
Go to:

christthekinglibrary.com

CKL
Christ The King Library